The Pilgrims' Way

DEREK BRIGHT

21/9/22.

For Mandy, Jack & Joe

The Pilgrims' Way

FACT AND FICTION OF AN ANCIENT TRACKWAY

DEREK BRIGHT

The History Press

The Pilgrims' Way passes through the Kent Downs Area of Outstanding Natural Beauty (AONB) for much of its length. The Kent Downs is a nationally important and enchanting English landscape much valued by local communities. The contents of this book represent the views of the author and do not necessarily represent the views of the Kent Downs AONB Unit or Partnership.

For more information about the Kent Downs AONB please visit www.kentdowns.org.uk or call 01303 815 170.

All photographs, with the exception of maps and diagrams, are the work of Richard Brown. The photographic work of Richard Brown can be found at www.arjaybeephotography.co.uk

First published 2011

The History Press
The Mill, Brimscombe Port
Stroud, Gloucestershire, GL5 2QG
www.thehistorypress.co.uk

Reprinted 2011

British Library Cataloguing in Publication Data.
A catalogue record for this book is available from the British Library.

ISBN 978 0 7524 6085 7

Typesetting and origination by The History Press
Printed in Great Britain

Contents

Acknowledgements

The author would like to thank the following people and institutions for their help, time and encouragement during the research and production of this book.

In particular, I would like to acknowledge Dr Andrew Ashbee, Chairman of Snodland Historical Society and Honorary Curator of Snodland Millennium Museum, whose kind words and advice encouraged the initial submission of 'The Pilgrims' Way Revisited: The Use of the North Downs Main Trackways and the Medway Crossings by Medieval Travellers' for publication and review as an e-article for the Kent Archaeological Society. I would also like to thank him for his time and knowledge given regarding road routes and river crossings in the Snodland area. Thanks must go also to Terence Lawson, Honorary Editor of the Kent Archaeological Society, for editing the original paper.

I am also indebted to the many friends who have walked sections of the Pilgrims' Way with me during the course of researching the book, including Adrian Madden, Jack Bright and Richard Brown. Also Anthony Gowers, Nick Gilbert, Mandy Bright, Alex Oehring and Cathy Peckham, Steve Ford-Elliot and Joe Bright, who have all freely given much time walking the Pilgrims' Way over the years. Moreover, the author acknowledges the help rendered over the years by Anthony Gowers, North Downs Way National Trail Officer, for his help in many matters in connection with the National Trail and the Pilgrims' Way.

I am grateful to the many people who kindly sent me their articles and papers, upon request and often at very short notice. These include: Dr Stuart Brookes, Dr Sue Harrington and Dr Andrew Reynolds with regard to the Archaeology of the Channel Tunnel Rail Link; David Calow, David Weston, and the Hampshire Field Club and Archaeological Society, including Dick Selwood, Julia Sandison and also Jenny Ruthven at the University of

Southampton, Hartley Library; Dr Andy Russel, Archaeology Unit Manager, Southampton Archaeology Unit, for his help regarding Richard of Southwick; Hannah Jeffery MCLIP Assistant Librarian, Surrey Archaeological Society, Guildford Museum, for advice and access to the Edwin Hart Collection. Thanks must also go to all those at the Centre for Kentish Studies, Kent Archive and Local History Service and, in particular, Deborah Saunders for her help and advice regarding early maps of Kent. The author also acknowledges the kind permission of the Centre for Kentish Studies to reproduce sections of maps owned by Kent County Council.

I am especially grateful to Sarah Loftus both for her encouragement and support during the last few years in connection with matters related to tourism and walking in the Kent Downs Area of Outstanding Natural Beauty, and remain indebted to her for the time she has given undertaking the initial proofreading of this book.

Finally, I have greatly appreciated the energy of Richard Brown, who has brought his own photographic style to the project and has spent many hours both walking and in his studio to capture the essence of the Pilgrims' Way on camera.

Foreword

Upon becoming the officer responsible for the North Downs Way National Trail, it soon became apparent to me that the trail had inherited a history that preceded its own inception in 1978. Much of the National Trail's route either follows or tracks closely the route known as the Pilgrims' Way or Pilgrims' Road. The National Trail's website invites walkers to follow in the footsteps of pilgrims on an inspirational journey, steeped in history, which passes through both the Surrey Hills and Kent Downs Areas of Outstanding Natural Beauty. For those planning the pilgrimage walk between Winchester and Canterbury, we recommend that walkers follow the St Swithun's Way to Farnham and then the North Downs Way to Canterbury.

It is the trail's link with the past that undoubtedly resonates with many that come to walk it each year and people come from all over the world to follow the trail to Canterbury. Yet so much of the history that has become associated with the way remains confused and unclear to many that enjoy what it has to offer. This is only too clear from the questions I am asked on a regular basis by people as they plan their own long-distance walk, the most common being 'what is the difference between the North Downs Way and the Pilgrims' Way?' In many places the National Trail follows what are believed to be some of the earliest trackways along the North Downs taken by prehistoric people, long before the days of medieval pilgrimage. The trail's connection with such a broad range of human travel throughout the course of history is one reason that makes exploration of the North Downs Way National Trail so attractive. It is also why those who enjoy walking the trail often raise questions about its past.

It is the North Downs Way National Trail's inextricable link with the Pilgrims' Way which for me makes this book so welcome. It reappraises the story of the Pilgrims' Way and delves deep into its history. It discerns the fact from the fiction and the myth from reality. In doing so, it reminds readers of the contributions made by Hilaire Belloc and Julia Cartwright, the Victorian and Edwardian writers who brought the Pilgrims' Way to the attention of a much larger audience. Also highlighted are some of the most recent archaeological finds and how they impact on our knowledge and understanding of the Pilgrims' Way. The book is also not afraid of dispelling some of the folklore associated with the way, where it is seen to be unsustainable.

The author's passion for the subject has been shared with the many walkers for whom he has organised walking holidays along the Pilgrims' Way. It is his enthusiasm, combined with this mass of evidence which Derek Bright has brought together in one volume, that allows the reader to connect with the past and experience their own inspirational journey along this ancient trackway.

Tony Gowers
North Downs Way National Trail Officer
February 2011

Introduction

A Hidden Byway
Through Time

Winding a course across the southern counties of Hampshire, Surrey and Kent, between Winchester and Canterbury, can be found what many believe to be one of England's most ancient trackways. Well trodden and beloved of walkers, this old road, better known to most as the Pilgrims' Way, still serves as a hidden byway through time, which rewards those that take the time and trouble to journey along it with a portal into the country's past. Today, tourists from all over the world come to walk the Pilgrims' Way, in whole or part, and its associations with Thomas Becket and medieval pilgrimage still have a resonance that spreads far and wide. Contemporary pilgrims usually choose to use the well-maintained and clearly way-marked North Downs Way National Trail, stopping overnight in inns and guest houses found along the wayside. Yet, in spite of its popularity, this highway across southern England remains an enigma to many who follow its tracks.

Elliston-Erwood described this intriguing mixture of myth and reality that surrounds the Pilgrims' Way in an article published in the *Archaeologia Cantiana*, in 1925, when he wrote:

> There is probably no other road or trackway in the whole of England that can boast such a literature as does this path, around which myth, legend, history, enthusiasm, and tradition have combined to weave such a tangled web. Running as it does through some of the most charming parts of the south country, Hampshire, Surrey, and Kent, generally on the southern slope of the chalk hills, but at times traversing ploughed fields, along deep sandy hollow ways or through gloomy yew-lined avenues, it can be followed from Winchester and the West to Canterbury and the coast.[1]

It is now nearly 500 years since Thomas Cromwell's and Cranmer's contribution to the Protestant Reformation effectively put an end to pilgrimage to Becket's shrine. Together with the abolition of saints days and the display of relics, a new personal relationship between man and god was forged, which precluded a role for intermediaries such as Saint Thomas. So as to ensure that no room remained for confusion, decrees were issued to eradicate all memory of Becket's existence to the extent that his name was removed from records, his image forbidden, and his bones removed and the shrine destroyed.[2]

Yet today many still come to walk the Pilgrims' Way and visit Canterbury. Of these modern-day pilgrims, many seek a deeper secular or spiritual meaning from their journey. For the journey can fulfil a basic human need for elemental feelings, which Hilaire Belloc recognised in the opening passages of the *The Old Road*, when he wrote: 'we craved these things – the camp, the refuge, the sentinels in the dark, the hearth – before we made them; they are part of our human manner, and when this civilisation has perished they will reappear. Of these primal things the least obvious and most important is The Road.'[3]

Popular folklore lays claim to the Pilgrims' Way as the path taken by thousands of medieval pilgrims to Becket's shrine, following his murder on 29 December 1170, until the arrival in Canterbury of the Royal Commission for the Destruction of Shrines, led by Dr Leyton in September 1538. There are, however, other voices that will assert that not a single pilgrim ever strode the ancient trackway along the edge of the North Downs en route to Becket's shrine. Although there is far less doubt amongst historians about the Pilgrims' Way (or certainly large sections of it) having prehistoric origins, more open to question is its use as a route of medieval pilgrimage to Canterbury.

From its prehistoric origins through to the romanticism of Victorian and Edwardian pilgrims, one will find a mass of contradictory views about how we should define the Pilgrims' Way. For the many who enjoy walking the way; for the countless numbers of people who live close to it; for those whose work brings them into daily contact with it; or those of us who simply have an awareness of the Way as a familiar historic feature within their locality – such a lack of clarity about the history of the Pilgrims' Way can but detract from the full enjoyment of it. In many quarters, the Pilgrims' Way has been politely left in a form of limbo, shown on maps in books but not directly referred to. The *persona non grata* of ancient trackways, widely acknowledged but best not mentioned. However, for its longevity alone, the narrative of the Pilgrims' Way merits both re-examination and reappraisal. This is particularly the case when one considers that the renowned historian of ancient trackways and Roman roads, Ivan Margary, once described the Pilgrims' Way as one of the most important ancient trackways in Britain.[4]

1 Pre-reformation murals of saints, St Lawrence church, Alton

2 North Tower with fireplaces, Archbishop's Palace, Otford

The story of the Pilgrims' Way and how we interpret it, like all subjects with a historical lineage, continues to evolve as has the trackway's adaptation and use over the passage of time. In the last century, long stretches of the Pilgrims' Way were incorporated into the North Downs Way. This long-distance footpath is one of fifteen national trails established by the Countryside Commission throughout England and Wales after the Second World War as part of the government's effort to open up rural access and recreation for people living in urban areas. Today, the North Downs Way National Trail comes under the auspices of Natural England and the two county councils through which it passes. The trackway still holds an integral role within many of the rural communities found along its route, serving as a public right of way in the various forms of public footpath, bridleway or byway open to all traffic (BOAT). In a number of places it still maintains a status as a public highway, albeit of a minor nature. Today, the trackway's raison d'être is primarily as a leisure amenity, owing much to the laudable post-war aims espoused in the National Parks & Access to the Countryside Act of 1949. Nevertheless, a broad economic rationale for its existence can still be found within the rural economy in the many farms, inns and small businesses situated along the way.

Any reappraisal of the ancient trackway must draw from the work of writers who, over the previous two centuries, have postulated various theories about the Pilgrims' Way. Writers such as Hilaire Belloc and Julia Cartwright (aka Mrs Ady), who wrote the first comprehensive accounts of the Pilgrims' Way and, in so doing, undoubtedly introduced it to a wider audience; the archaeologists and antiquarians such as Captain H.W. Knocker, F.C. Elliston-Erwood, Wilfrid Hooper, C.G. Crump and Edwin Hart, who debated the merits of the Pilgrims' Way in the pages of publications such as *Archaeologia Cantiana*, the *Surrey Archaeological Collections* and the *Hampshire Field Club Newsletters*; the cartographers such as Captain E.R. James and Andrews, Dury and Herbert, who put the trackway on the maps; the authors of the county histories such as Edward Brayley, Robert Furley and Manning and Bray, who included the Pilgrims' Way in their accounts of the shires; and the nineteenth-century essayist Grant Allen, who sought to mythologise the Pilgrims' Way as the great trackway across southern England from the West Country in an Arcadian past.

Through an assessment of the numbers within the population at liberty to leave the medieval manor and take to the road, it is possible to place the road's usage in a more realistic context. Whilst today's walkers enjoy retracing Belloc's 'old road', we should ask ourselves how many of us would have been going on an extended pilgrimage if we had been living in the Middle Ages.

In consideration of the everyday hazards faced by wayfarers in the past, we need to reappraise how the road has served travellers over time. How did roadside crime affect the medieval traveller and to what extent did the dangers faced by travellers on the road determine the routes they chose to take? Would pilgrims avoid centres of population and, if so, why did some places present greater risks than others? What prompted legislation to be introduced that prohibited medieval travel and how did this impact upon pilgrimage? Today we may judge pilgrimage as a benign pastime, yet directives were issued to prevent people going on pilgrimage who did not possess the means to support themselves, and monarchs at various times throughout the Middle Ages often viewed pilgrimage as an act of political defiance and a challenge to their authority.

We also need to consider the development of ideas critical of pilgrimage and the growth of anti-pilgrimage sentiment expressed by some medieval writers and the effect this had upon popular notions of pilgrimage at the time. Only once we have an awareness of issues such as these, and the questions they raise, can we begin to redefine the history of the Pilgrims' Way for the thousands who walk it each year, enabling us to place our own experience of the way within a credible and realistic context.

The modern-day pilgrim will see numerous road signs on their journey, constantly reinforcing the veracity of the Pilgrims' Way. Many signs, such as the ones made of pressed tin and enamelled with embossed scallop shells depicting the sign of St James, can be seen frequently by the wayside. Medieval houses bearing names of Pilgrims' Lodge or Pilgrims' Cottage suggest a historic lineage to the road we follow. Timber-framed inns and restaurants display names such as the Pilgrims' Rest or have adopted the names of Chaucerian characters to remind us of those who preceded the footsteps of contemporary travellers. Local products bear brand names derived from medieval pilgrimage, embracing history in an attempt to affirm certainty of their authenticity and continuity with the past. Today's walker also has well way-marked routes to follow, with Ordnance Survey maps that show the trail with sections of the Pilgrims' Way as 'Trackway' depicted in Old English typeface.

Today's travellers will meet local people who will often volunteer what appears to be a snippet of local folklore. As is so often the case when one is walking, local people are pleased to share their understanding about their locality and its history with those who take the time and trouble to walk and show an interest. They may well tell you about pilgrims leaving the original Roman snails that can still be found along the trackway today near Charing; or the pilgrims' porch where they gathered to find safety in numbers from robbers before ascending into the dark depths of King's Wood; or the lines of yews that mark the way on the hillside; or the first view that pilgrims got of the Bell Harry Tower of Canterbury Cathedral as the way emerges from the shelter of the woods above Godmersham.

3 Kent County Council's Pilgrims' Way sign, Chilham village

But as Oliver Rackham, the historian of the English countryside, warns: beware of factoids. Pseudo-history is made up of factoids. A factoid looks like a fact, is respected as a fact, and has all the properties of a fact except that it is not true.

So as we make our way to Canterbury, we must beware of factoids in an eagerness to find the Pilgrims' Way. On the journey one will also meet those who will pronounce that the Pilgrims' Way is simply a construct that exists in the imaginative minds of Victorian and Edwardian authors; or others who will tell you that we are merely using Saxon drovers' trails and farm tracks, connected together by the over enthusiasm of a few antiquarians. Of course, you may also meet modern-day pilgrimists who will gladly share with you what they believe to be the evidence of pilgrimage scattered along the Way between Winchester and Canterbury. The following chapters explore much of the evidence both for and against the theories of the Way. It's a backpackers' guide to the history of the 'old road' that attempts to discern fact from fiction, myth from reality. Its aim is to equip those who walk the Pilgrims' Way with the background, from which to make their own judgement – which, of course, we can never entirely separate from a subjective view of our own history. However, one should always bear in mind that even factoids weren't created in a vacuum and are often simply the product of ordinary people trying to make sense of their own history.

1

The Pilgrims' Way in the Landscape

The Prehistoric Migration Route

Somewhat surprisingly, the story of the Pilgrims' Way commences neither at Winchester, which is the start of the 'old road' and the medieval monarchical capital of the Anglo-Saxon kings, nor from its final destination of Canterbury and the centre of English Christianity. Instead, the story of the Pilgrims' Way begins a few miles south of Canterbury at the Channel coast near Dover. And it is a story, the heart of which is inextricably linked to chalk.

Each time we cross the English Channel from mainland Europe, it is chalk that dominates the approach to Dover and our return to England's shores. As we cast an eye back toward Cap Gris Nez and the distant shoreline of the French coast, it is chalk that serves to remind us that throughout much of human history, Kent's physical connection to the continental land mass was not by water but by chalk. A great swathe of chalk downland that had once linked Britain with the European continental land mass. The very same chalk from which is derived the earliest name given to Britain: Albion, 'meaning white, bestowed on the island by the great sea-captain Pytheas sailing from Marseilles in the fourth century BC'.[1]

The Straits are but a narrow breach in the chalk, broken and worn by the combined forces of the North Sea and the Atlantic, which left exposed the White Cliffs at Dover and the Cap Blanc Nez at the Pay-de-Calais. Today, the ferry and Channel Tunnel serve as a bridge, linking this immense belt of chalk downland, which runs from the Bas-Boulonnais area of northern France, with Kent. From here the chalk sweeps west in two broad bands across southern England to converge on Salisbury Plain, before finally radiating over Wiltshire and south through Dorset as far as the Purbeck Hills. The same band of chalk, which overshadows the old port town of Dover, remains a recurrent theme throughout this story and central to our appreciation and understanding of the Pilgrims' Way.

Yet this chalk massif dramatically halts at the Kent coast, presenting a perpendicular wall, salami-sliced by the North Sea, to plunge more than 100 metres to the shoreline below. Along 10 miles of coastline, from Folkestone in the west to Walmer in the east, this wall of chalk appears to offer a formidable barrier to any further advance inland. But in reality these cretaceous beds of sedimentary chalk have served as the migratory route into Britain from mainland Europe for many thousands of years. Archaeological evidence suggests that, at various times during the last 500,000 years, during cold cycles, when vast amounts of the earth's water became held in glaciers, sea levels were lower and southern Britain tilted slightly upwards due to the immense weight of the ice caps, hominines made the journey north across the chalk land bridge linking Dover and Calais. Such a land bridge is described by Francis Wenban-Smith, when he states: 'there would have been a highway of chalk downland, rich in flint raw material for tool manufacture and grazed by abundant herbivores, leading along the north eastern side of the Wealden anticline and continuing into what has been described as northern France.'[2]

At different times, this route was most likely taken by pre-Neanderthal, Neanderthal and later modern human hunter-gatherers in a continued process that has been described as one of colonisation, abandonment and recolonisation of Britain. Valerie Belsey, in *The Green Lanes of England*, suggests that the earliest tracks along the North Downs escarpment date back to a time when man hunted along tracks used by wild animals.

Far more recently, the chalk route to Britain was the one taken by Mesolithic (middle Stone Age) and Neolithic (late Stone Age) explorers, hunters and traders, who crossed once again from the main European land mass.[3] With the retreat of the last ice age some 10,000 years ago, sea levels remained lower and the land bridge remained exposed.[4] However, around 8300 years ago, as the glaciers retreated still further and Britain once again became separated for the final time, the rising waters of the North Sea cut through the chalk linking Kent and northern France.[5] Between 5500 and 3500 years before the present day, the Kent coastline would have started to resemble the one we are familiar with today.

Yet, despite the loss of the land bridge, the inhabitants of Kent continued to maintain links with mainland Europe through sea travel across the Channel.[6] There is no better evidence of this than the Dover Bronze Age boat, estimated to be 3600 years old. The boat was discovered by construction workers in 1992, when a shaft for a storm water pump was being dug in Dover town centre.[7] The boat, whose full length archaeologists estimate to have been between 12 and 18 metres, is now preserved and on display at the Bronze Age

Boat Gallery in Dover Museum, close to where it was discovered. Perhaps most fittingly, the boat is preserved for posterity at the end of the chalk ridge, close to the trail marker that signifies the finish of the North Downs Way National Trail on the esplanade at Dover. It is thought that such a vessel may have had a crew of 16 paddlers with 4 crewmen acting as bailers and a capability of carrying a cargo of 3 tonnes across the Channel on a calm day.[8]

But the Dover Bronze Age boat is far from being an isolated example of evidence supporting prehistoric sea travel and European trade. Divers discovered Bronze Age cargo, lost at sea around 3000 years ago at Langdon Bay (adjacent to the port of Dover), which is believed to originate from a ship that foundered while attempting to enter the Dour Estuary.[9] Furthermore, the significant increase in metalwork recorded in Kent from the Early to Late Bronze Age suggests 'wealth derived from participation in an increasingly cosmopolitan world'.[10]

Central to the Pilgrims' Way story is the relationship between chalk and human travel. Rather than being an impenetrable barrier between the British Isles and the Continent, the reality is that throughout most of human existence the very same chalk that forms the White Cliffs of Dover has been an aid to human migration into Britain. And later, in warmer periods when the land bridge became submerged, it was the Straits that offered the shortest distance for early mariners to cross between the Kent coast and the northern European mainland, aided by the visibility of the towering chalk on either coastline, which offered an early navigation aid.

The Chalk Escarpment

At Dover the Pilgrims' Way story really begins, for here we meet the geological feature that, more than any other, defines the Pilgrims' Way. As Dan Tuson informs us in his recent study of the Kent Downs, it is at this 'most easterly point, where the huge mass of the North Downs is exposed in cross section as the majestic White Cliffs of Dover and Folkestone; the escarpment begins its journey'.

This chalk escarpment's relationship with human travel is aptly summed up by Tuson when he describes it as 'A sweeping arc leading through from the Channel coast to the heartland of southern England, its natural accessibility has bestowed upon it an attraction and appeal as a journey and trade route for centuries'.[11]

Today's travellers, once disembarked at the port of Dover, can progress inland by road to Canterbury, a journey which cuts a path up through the chalk to ascend on to the rolling plateaux of the North Downs above. Alternatively, as a port town, there had long been a breach in the chalk downland cut by the River Dour on its course to the sea, which was the route chosen by the Roman road builders and is the route taken by the railway today.

However, the route most likely favoured by prehistoric travellers exploited the inherent benefits offered by the chalk escarpment. There was good reason for this as the chalk scarp, steering as it does a course westward along the edge of the Downs, offered both firm yet porous qualities and was mixed with flint. Not only was the going good underfoot, the south-facing escarpment soaked up the sun for most of the day and, as such, remained dry. More than any other geological feature, it is this protruding outcrop of chalk, which for 125 miles flanks the edge of the North Downs between Dover and Farnham, that defines the Pilgrims' Way. It is described by Dr Peter Brandon in his book which captures his life-long passion for the North Downs, as 'The great glory of the North Downs is its escarpment which faces south into the sun, unlike the corresponding escarpment of the South Downs, and in consequence, a kind of "inland Riviera" prevails, where, sheltered by the undercliff, is the finest human habitat in southern England'.[12]

These exposed upper and middle layers of chalk, formed by the build-up of minute fossilised sea creatures that came to rest on the sea bed, were laid down over millions of years. The solidified layers of sedimentary rock presented pre-historic travellers with an efficient route by which they could progress inland. Chalk was therefore both an instrumental and determining influence on the movement of early travellers upon their arrival in Kent.

The prominence of this sweeping ridge of chalk across southern England was captured by some of the earliest cartographers of Kent. John Speed's animated maps, which include the County of Kent, published in 1611, exag-geratingly depict this ridge of chalk bordering the North Downs as a range of 43 mountainous peaks stretching across the county from 'Folkston' to 'Tatsfield', and on through Surrey. Without doubt, Speed wanted to empha-sise to his public the significance of this geological feature, how it dominated Kent, separating the county from north to south, cutting across as it does east to west. Interestingly, Symonson's map of Kent, produced in 1596, which preceded Speed's map and was published widely by Stent in 1650, similarly depicts the chalk ridge as a mountainous band running through the middle of the county.[13]

Two hundred years later, the famous diarist and social commentator William Cobbett, like John Speed, conveyed to his readers the recurring presence of the chalk escarpment in his travels through the Kent and Sussex landscape in the pages of *Rural Rides*. As Cobbett looked down over the Weald of Kent from the crest of the ridge above Hollingbourne, his account for the Friday evening of 5 September 1823 recalls how 'all of a sudden, I found myself upon the edge of a hill, as lofty and as steep as that at Folkestone, at Reigate, or at Ashmansworth. It was the same famous chalk ridge that I was crossing again.'[14]

A Route Westward Across Southern England

The footprints of contemporary travellers continue to leave their mark along the ancient chalk trackways of the southern flank of the North Downs. For Winchester- or Canterbury-bound walkers following the course of the Pilgrims' Way over the Downs between the medieval town of Farnham and the city of Canterbury, it is the acorn symbols of the North Downs Way National Trail that mark today's route of choice. Most walkers allow between 10 and 14 days, giving them time to explore the rural backwaters and hidden byways between the two cathedral cities. Between Winchester and Farnham, today's walkers opt to follow the way-marked St Swithun's Way along the valleys of the River Wey and the River Itchen. A visitor survey undertaken by the North Downs Way National Trails' Project in 2004 showed that the trail is still well used today and found that between May and October 250,000 people used the trail.

At the eastern end of the trail some walkers choose to include the section of the Pilgrims' Way that continues further east beyond the market town of

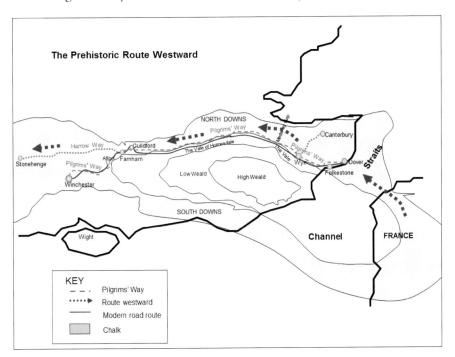

4 The prehistoric route westward

Wye, rather than take the Stour Valley north-east for the last 15 miles to arrive at Canterbury. This option continues along the edge of the Kent Downs, on to Dover, following in the footsteps of prehistoric travellers. Much of this section has also been incorporated into the North Downs Way loop.

However, at this point in the Pilgrims' Way story it is useful to examine the route westwards from the Kent coast and the port of Dover. Taking a few moments to understand how the contemporary road traveller, with only hours rather than days to spare, undertakes the journey westward may offer some clues about how our ancestors undertook such a journey.

Today, it is the M20 motorway that offers the modern traveller a route to the west across southern England. Driving out of the old port town of Dover, situated at the base of the cliffs, with its formidable castle and succession of Napoleonic defences towering above, one can track the journey taken by prehistoric travellers thousands of years ago. Unlike the hidden landscape for the walker to discover along the ridge paths, terrace-ways and holloways of the North Downs, the motorway adopts a course parallel to the southern foothills of the escarpment, keeping to the lower ground of the vale.

After journeying 10 miles west, the road route takes us past the town of Folkestone. Here the chalk escarpment turns inland, gradually at first, and away from the county's southern coastline. The motorway does likewise, still maintaining a course parallel to the hillside and ever moving west. For the next 30 miles the modern highway never attempts to ascend the chalk escarpment on to the North Downs above, content to navigate a steady path along the foot of the hills in the vale below and steering well south of the numerous little spring-line villages nestling at the foot of the chalk. As we have seen, unlike today's motorist, the prehistoric traveller remained on the hillside, keeping to the firm chalk underfoot, rather than venturing out into softer soil, of what would later become the rich agricultural belt of the vale.

As the ruins of Boxley's medieval abbey are passed, our course westward has now tracked the hillside to the right for a distance of almost 50 miles. The abbey, much of which was transferred to the Wyatt family upon the dissolution of the monasteries, after Thomas Cromwell's infamous showpiece exposé of monastic cunning and greed, became a cause célèbre of the Reformation. After passing Boxley abbey we reach the second of two natural gaps in the chalk scarp. These interruptions in the chalk are wide valley mouths, which in effect are but enormous funnels marking the confluence of the gathering tributaries from the watersheds in the Weald, whereupon they muster enough force to cut corridors through the chalk downland to reach the Kent coastal plains and the Thames Estuary. The first of these breaks in the chalk scarp is the breach cut by the River Stour on its way to Canterbury and the second and much wider breach is known as the Medway Gap. The diagram on page 23

5 Coldrum stones looking towards Medway Gap, with chalk escarpment to left

plots both the modern course of the M20 motorway and the route taken by prehistoric travellers westward from the Straits of Dover.

In the Medway Gap, not only do we find evidence of prehistoric settlers that may have been frequent users of the North Downs trackways, but we also find a concentration of the structures that they built to house their dead. These megaliths of sarsen stone are the remains of the architecture that formed numerous long barrows, and include Kits Coty House, Lower Kits Coty House, the Coffin Stone, Warren Farm and the White Horse Stone, situated east of the River Medway; and the Coldrum Stones, the Chestnuts and the Addington Stones, situated on the west bank of the Medway.[15] The structures are particularly unusual for the enormity of their chambers. It is also noteworthy that this small area had the highest density of such structures found in the south of England outside of Salisbury Plain. Paul Ashbee noted that: 'The Kentish sarsen stones, mostly upon Blue Bell Hill were, as they are now sorely depleted, the largest southern English concentration of such stones, apart from Northern Wiltshire.'[16]

This is far from the only area that has abundant evidence of the Neolithic (the first Stone Age farmers) and evidence of much earlier human activity close to the chalk downland has been found. There is an increasing appreciation that early human activity close to the North Downs was far more common than previously thought. Francis Wenban-Smith points to the importance of the monuments in the Medway and Stour valleys when he says:

> The Medway and Stour long-barrows, though familiar monuments in the local landscape, are some of the least known and most seldom cited in wider debates on the British Neolithic. Yet they should be some of the most important. Despite their present ruinous condition and unimpressive condition, they were some of the largest and most impressive monuments of the British Neolithic, especially in the size of their sarsen chambers. Whatever explanation is adopted for the origins of agriculture in Britain, the beginning of the Neolithic involved the undisputed innovations from the Continent: the domesticated cereals and sheep were not indigenous. Kent, as the British side of the shortest crossing, must have played a significant role.[17]

As the M20 motorway continues west, it strikes a 9-mile course across the Medway Gap, where the valley is at its widest point between Boxley and Trottiscliffe, just south of the marshes and the medieval town of Aylesford. Between the Medway Gap and the end of the escarpment at Farnham, the chalk is breached a further three times by the river valleys of the Darenth, Mole and the Wey, each succeeding in their quest to join with the waters of the Thames and the North Sea.

After Trottiscliffe, the line of chalk again draws closer to the motorway until the modern highway reasserts its distance from the escarpment, keeping to the hundred-metre contour line rather than climbing the ridge. Journeying further westward, we pass the spring-line villages of Wrotham, Kemsing and Otford in the Vale of Holmesdale, set between the two parallel geological features of the ridge of greensand to the south and the chalk scarp flanking the Downs to the north. At Chevening, the M20 and M25 motorways converge and the route to the West Country now joins the M25 corridor, which carves a scar through the fertile agricultural soils of the vale.

6 Exposed cross-section of chalk downland near Folkstone

Upon passing Reigate, our journey has now taken a course of 70 miles since leaving Dover. The motorway now challenges the chalk scarp, climbing towards the ridge for the first time since leaving the Kent coastline, ascending the hundred or so metres to the top of the scarp and the North Downs beyond. But here we leave the M25 and take its older predecessor, the A25, the road to Guildford and once the turnpike road, which remains compliant as it keeps a westbound direction through the Vale of Holmesdale.

At the village of Shere the old toll road leaves the vale and it too ascends the chalk scarp, and our modern road journey west crosses the Pilgrims' Way for the first time since leaving Dover before we enter Guildford, above Albury Downs. Beyond Guildford, the A31, which too was an old turnpike road, takes us a further 11 miles to the town of Farnham, via the Hog's Back, the distinctive geological feature where the scarp takes the form of a thin chalk spine. The ridge of the Hog's Back drops away either side, offering broad panoramas across the Puttenham Vale and the Surrey Hills. The renowned expert on ancient roads, Ivan Margary, referred to man's passage along the top of this outcrop of chalk when he wrote that the 'Hog's Back is an ideal example of a ridge way with the open grassy topped ridge falling away in steep slopes on both sides'.[18]

Today it is the car and the road that monopolises the chalk ridge over the high ground of the Hog's Back, whereas it is the Pilgrims' Way that, according to Belloc, makes its way by descending to the belt of greensand and sandy soil in the Vale of Puttenham. Whilst the modern highway heads for Farnham

7 King Alfred sculpture in
St Bartholomew's Church,
Winchester

along the ridge, Belloc's 'old road' passes below on a course close to the village
of Compton, through the village of Puttenham, across Puttenham Heath and
on through Seale.

Upon reaching the medieval town of Farnham our journey brings us close
to Winchester, the starting point of the Pilgrims' Way. From Farnham it is less
than a 30-minute journey by car to Winchester and less than two days' walk.
If we wished to complete our journey here we are within 30 miles of the old
capital of Wessex and the Anglo-Saxon kings. But it is at this point that the
Pilgrims' Way story has an important twist. Moreover, it's a twist that cannot
be ignored if its prehistoric origins are to be properly understood.

Throughout the course of the modern road journey we have observed how
the Pilgrims' Way has kept, for the most part, well to the north and close to
or up upon the chalk hillside. The ancient trackway has kept well away from
today's road route, avoiding both the claggy clay of the Vale of Holmesdale
to its south and the forest of the Weald of Kent and Sussex beyond. The road
journey has tracked the progress of the Pilgrims' Way from a distance, keeping
to the lower soft and fertile soils of vale. Nevertheless, this modern route
is significant because, as can be seen from the diagram on page 23, it still
essentially adopts the route taken by prehistoric travellers on their passage

across southern England. Geological features have continued to determine the course of our modern arterial roads from Dover through to the west of the country. The route around the southern section of the M25 motorway, London's great orbital highway, takes the motorist on a journey not too dissimilar to the one undertaken by countless prehistoric travellers upon arriving in Kent and heading westward.

Maybe many of today's travellers have much in common with their prehistoric counterparts that used the route thousands of years ago. Perhaps some share similar reasons for making the journey west: pushed by circumstances to become economic or political migrants; to carry out the day-to-day requirements of trading relationships; or even to undertake a pilgrimage to a place that held a wider significance for people beyond their locality.

Belloc and *The Old Road*

Today's highway to the West Country from Dover, with its proximity to the North Downs escarpment, still has in essence tracked the modern equivalent of the route that served as the building block for Hilaire Belloc's seminal work about the Pilgrims' Way. Entitled *The Old Road* and published in 1904, like our modern journey, Belloc's 'old road' started neither at Winchester nor Canterbury, but commenced at Dover. Irrespective of whether one agrees with all of Belloc's theories about the Pilgrims' Way, his account was the most influential of the Victorian and Edwardian writers on the subject. Of all the early writers, Ivan Margary regarded Belloc's *The Old Road* as the 'best known and most important contribution'.[19] Belloc is regularly accredited as the author of the first authoritative account of the Pilgrims' Way. But, in fact, he was neither the first nor certainly the last writer on the subject. Very few references are made to the Pilgrims' Way without alluding to Belloc. Perhaps a 'pivotal account' would be a better way of describing the role of Belloc's *The Old Road*.

Belloc's work, irrespective of its popularity, was certainly not the first to examine the history and folklore pertaining to the supposed pilgrimage route that traced an ancient trackway across Hampshire, Kent and Surrey. It is worth noting that Belloc chose not to use the term "Pilgrims' Way" himself and seldom mentioned it by name, preferring to refer to the North Downs trackways as either the 'Way' or the 'Road'.

Belloc's theory of how geological features determined the route used by prehistoric travellers is set out in the second chapter of *The Old Road*. It is here that Belloc outlines how an ancient trackway ran across southern England and emphasises the central role of the south-facing chalk scarp bordering the edge of the North Downs when he states that:

A man who should leave the straits with the object of reaching the Hampshire centres would find a moderately steep, dry, chalky slope, always looking full towards the southern sun, bare of trees, cut but the three river valleys (and but one of these of any width), not often indented with combes or projecting spurs: this conspicuous range would lead him by the mere view of it straight on to his destination.[20]

The Harroway and Stonehenge

Here, then, is the first twist in the Pilgrims' Way story, because at Farnham, Belloc's prehistoric travellers did not forsake the chalk for the valleys of the River Wey and the Itchen and make for the area around Winchester. Instead, Belloc argues that they kept to the chalk on the higher ground and from Farnham took an ancient trackway that has become known as the Harroway or Hoar Way. The derivation of the name varies greatly depending upon who you refer to. Timperley and Brill suggest it is one of the oldest roads in Britain and refer to it as the Harrow or 'Hard Way'.[21] Jacetta Hawkes believed it to be one of the main east–west thoroughfares used by prehistoric man. An article by Viscountess Hanworth and F.A. Hastings published in the *Surrey Archaeological Collections* cites Crawford from *Archaeology in the Field*, who goes as far as suggesting that Harroway is derived from 'Heargweg', the 'shrine way', or the way to Stonehenge.[22]

It is the Harroway that took Belloc's prehistoric travellers westward towards Salisbury Plain and Stonehenge. For Salisbury Plain is where all the great chalk ridges of southern England converge and Belloc is far from alone in the view that the Harroway served as a key east–west trackway that extended across southern England. The centrality of Salisbury Plain, in terms of the trackways that early travellers followed, is summarised by Timperley and Brill in *Ancient Trackways of Wessex* when they wrote:

> Crossing and reaching outward from Salisbury Plain the trackways led along the hills to the ports and estuaries of the North Sea and Channel Coasts; to the Severn estuary, to the Cotswolds and the Midlands beyond. These tracks were literally highways because they were the watershed ways that only descended to cross even a small valley when there was no practicable line around the hilltops on the other side.[23]

Belsey, in *Green Lanes of England*, refers to the Harroway as one of 'the principal prehistoric trackways, believed to date from before 2000 BC', and lists these as being: the Harroway, the Ridgeway, the Icknield Way and the North and

South Downs Ridgeways.[24] Belloc is clearly of the view that the great mega-lithic sites of Stonehenge and Avebury on the Salisbury chalk plateau are the final destination of the road that ran from the Straits of Dover to the west, and states that 'these continuous high lands would present the first natural high-ways by which a primitive people could gather from all parts of the island'.[25]

It is beyond the scope of this reappraisal to speculate at any length as to the significance that the great henges held in the lives of these early travellers or the veracity of claims that they were the final destinations of the princi-pal chalk routes. That a word of caution should be exercised is suggested by Christopher Taylor in *Roads and Tracks of Britain*, when he states that 'Finally in this examination of Neolithic trackways we must note the routes which led to the great "temples" of this period. These huge constructions must have brought worshippers from near and far, but again their lines of approach are obscure.'[26]

In 2005 further evidence of the distances people travelled to visit the henges came to light when the remains of a young teenager were discovered outside Amesbury, close to Stonehenge. This burial find, which became known as the 'boy with the amber necklace', is believed to be about 3550 years old and tests undertaken by the British Geological Survey determined that the boy had probably travelled from a coastal Mediterranean area. It is thought that he may have come to Britain with an extended family on a grand tour. Andrew Fitzpatrick of Wessex Archaeology was reported as saying: 'We think that the wealthiest people may have made these long-distance journeys in order to source rare and exotic materials, like amber. By doing these journeys, they probably also acquired great kudos.'[27]

The boy with the amber necklace was not the first overseas traveller to have been located near Stonehenge and is but one of a number of burials in the area that provide evidence that prehistoric travellers covered considerable distance to visit the area.

Of course, it is pertinent to the Pilgrims' Way story that the seven Medway megaliths – the chambered tombs found close to the North Downs trackway in the Medway Valley – are also considered to be some of the most impor-tant of the British Neolithic.[28] Although these may be of earlier origin than the henge monuments of Salisbury Plain, it is interesting to note the sug-gestion that the Medway megaliths may also have held a wider significance than simply being burial sites, although archaeologists are still unsure of the meaning they held. As Tim Champion notes, their clustering is unusual and suggests 'it would argue against their interpretation as territorial markers for dispersed social groups, but would certainly suggest that particular locations had special meaning within the landscape'.[29] Killick argues that the Medway megaliths could indicate a particular importance of the area, and goes on to

8 Kits Coty House

state that 'this could be due to the prominent backdrop of the North Downs, the availability of resources from the Medway valley (not least the plentiful supply of sarsens) and the presence of established route ways along which Neolithic populations travelled'.[30] It is possible that there were prehistoric travellers using the North Downs trackways who were familiar with both the Wessex henges and the Medway megaliths.

The Harroway is certainly considered as a serious contender as one of the principal pre-Roman prehistoric trackways across southern England. As we have seen, some commentators refer to it as a continuous route linking with the North Downs trackways, i.e. the Pilgrims' Way. Cochrane, when describing the trackway's adoption in Roman Britain, states that 'the Harroway running from Dover in Kent to Ilchester in Somerset was one – may be the chief – of the east–west routes'.[31]

This, in effect, is how Hippisley-Cox made reference to the Pilgrims' Way in 1914. A chapter entitled 'Four Hampshire Roads' describes the Harrow Way or Hoar Way as a confluence of three ridge tracks meeting at Weyhill then running east to Ellisfield Camp. From here Hippisley-Cox suggests that the route took a 'course along the North Downs, following much the same direction as that taken in later days by the Pilgrims' Way'.[32]

Harold John Massingham, a prolific writer who had a great love of the English chalk downland, referred to the Harroway as the hoary track or Hoar Way and also described its route as a continuation of the Pilgrims' Way:

> Henceforward the pilgrims' road actually is the Hoar Way or Harroway, which has run into Chaucer's road all the way from Marazion in Cornwall, into Salisbury Plain, past the Neolithic camp at Yarnbury the Celts refortified fifteen centuries before, then leaves to Stonehenge and Amesbury. Beyond Amesbury, it leaves the ridgeway I followed by Quarley Hill and Danebury, and strikes, without passing any more villages above the gap between Doles Wood and Harewood Forest and right across Hampshire above the sources of the Test and the Lodden to Farnham.[33]

Notwithstanding Massingham's reference to Chaucer's road being incorrect, as Chaucer's pilgrims almost certainly travelled along Watling Street, his description of the Harroway is interesting in as much as it not only takes the Harroway beyond the area of the Henges and Salisbury Plain but also offers its origin as being at Marazion in Cornwall.

Early Trade Routes to and from the West

The view that a continuous prehistoric trackway followed the chalk and lime-stone beds across southern England is essential to the Pilgrims' Way story. That such a trackway existed is crucial to sustain not only Belloc's theory but a host of other pilgrimist writers who, as we have seen, argued that a Winchester to Canterbury trackway was in itself but a later adoption of the main prehistoric artery across southern England. However, such a view is not just depend-ent upon pushing the route further west into Wessex, beyond Farnham and past the end of the North Downs Ridge. To lend credibility to the view that there had been sustained Mesolithic and Neolithic travel along and beyond the chalk scarp, there also needed to be a reason for such journeys. And this reason was trade.

If prehistoric pioneers followed the trackways westward, it was the devel-opment of prehistoric trade that encouraged the use of the chalk routes as through-routes from the western counties, back and forth through Hampshire, Surrey and Kent, as far as the Channel crossings to the Continent.

Although the commencement of the Harroway at Marazion is not directly referred to by Belloc, he does suggest that an east–west route may have run as far as Cornwall. Julia Cartwright, writing a few years prior to the publica-tion of Belloc's *The Old Road*, also suggests that the old British track may have been, as some writers suppose, the road along which tin was transported from Cornwall and then shipped from east Kent. Sandwich, from where Cartwright suggests the tin was exported, overlooks the Straits and is only 16 miles due east of Dover. Cartwright claims Grant Allen as her source and it is Allen who, in his *Science of Arcady* published in 1892, suggests that:

> A very old trackway known as the Pilgrims Way, because it was followed in later times by medieval wayfarers from Somerset and Dorset to the shrine of St. Thomas a Beckett at Canterbury. But Mr. Charles Elton has shown conclusively that the Pilgrims' Way is many centuries more ancient than the martyr of King Henry's epoch, and it was used in the Bronze Age for the transport of tin from the mines in Cornwall to the port of Sandwich.[34]

But perhaps Grant Allen's *Science in Arcady* offers us more myth than real-ity when he describes how 'a very old trackway runs along the crest of the Downs from the West Country to Kent' along which 'Cornish tin was trans-ported by land across the whole breadth of southern Britain and shipped to the continent from the Isle of Thanet'.[35] In spite of Allen's claim that Charles Elton had shown conclusively that a route was used to transport tin from mines in Cornwall to Sandwich, there appears to be a lack of hard evidence in support of Allen's assertion that 'to this day antique ingots of valuable metal are often dug up in hoards or finds along the ancient track'.[36] Julia Cartwright repeats Allen's claim concerning the existence of such a trackway when she informed her readers that 'antiquarian researchers have abundantly proved this road to be an old British track, which was in use even before the coming of the Romans'.[37] She goes on to explain that this track 'may even have been, as some writers suppose, the road along which caravans of merchants brought their ingots of tin from Cornwall to be shipped at what was the great harbour of Britain, the Rutupine Port, afterwards Sandwich Haven, then borne overland to Massilia and the Mediterranean shores'.[38]

Elliston-Erwood, who eventually became increasingly critical of pilgrimist theory, recognised the necessity of a trackway taking the 'old road' westward to Salisbury Plain to support Belloc's theory, based upon the existence of a prehistoric east–west trackway, but declared 'the route taken by this track must remain unproven'. He was certainly dismissive of Grant Allen's tin trade theory and was quite categorical when he stated that 'whatever its course, it owes nothing to the metal traffic in early times'. Any such trade, he argued, was undertaken from the Wight, and adds that any ingots that have been found are either Roman or later.[39] Nevertheless, it is recognised by archaeologists that 'South-east England has no native source of copper or tin so all the metalwork found there must be made from imported materials'.[40] The similarities of Bronze Age graves in Wessex and Kent has been acknowledged, suggesting 'shared ideas and practices', although Champion states that communication by use of sea routes extending westward along the south coast would be reasonable to suppose.[41] Frank W. Jessup, referring to a slightly later period, states that:

> An indication of the main trade routes is given by the finds of single coins belonging to this period (i.e. pre-roman Iron Age). Most of the single coins that have been found were either on the line of the North Downs trackway, near the Thanet coast or along the banks of the Thames.[42]

But much earlier, about 8000 years ago, a particular type of siliceous rock, similar to flint found in southern England but only in the chert-bearing beds of limestone at Portland Bill, became a material of choice for making tools. Perhaps chert from Portland, which has been found as far afield as east Devon, Cornwall, Somerset, Hampshire, Surrey, Wiltshire and Gloucestershire, offers another motive for travel that is supported by better evidence. As Christopher Taylor noted: 'the chert tools from Surrey suggest that the ridgeway route along the North Downs, later to become known as the Pilgrims' Way, was a possible line taken by the chert traders.'[43]

The Winchester and Canterbury Hubs

The second twist to the Pilgrims' Way story is Belloc's introduction of new points of origin and departure at either end of the route. Having established an argument for a prehistoric east–west trade route, he then swaps Canterbury for Dover at the eastern end and Winchester for Stonehenge at the western end. Belloc's hypothesis was based on his view that, due to changing winds and tides, early mariners adopted a multiplicity of harbours. As such, in Kent this multiplicity of harbours included Lympne, Folkestone, Dover, Sandwich, Richborough, Ramsgate and Reculver. Belloc concludes that Canterbury developed essentially because it was approximately equidistant from the main Kentish ports; close to the tidal limit of the Stour and, as such, close to both a navigable passage to the sea and a source of fresh water. He cites both Caesar's landing at Deal and Augustine's landing at Richborough as evidence of the strategic importance that Canterbury had obtained by the late Iron Age.

Caesar landed at Deal, but Canterbury's fort was the place he had to take; Augustine landed at Richborough, but Canterbury was the place wherein he fixed the origins of Christianity in England.[44]

Belloc introduces the notion that changed the route at both ends and argues that this reflects the road's evolving character over time. At the western end, he introduces the theory of how Winchester supplants Stonehenge as the great Way's origin.[45] In effect, he supplants the Harrow Way at the western end in favour of his own theory that prehistoric travellers kept to the Vale of the River Itchen and then the Vale of the River Wey for the 30 miles between Winchester and Farnham.

At the eastern end he introduces Canterbury and a whole theory based upon the need for a hub that gave equidistance access to the Kent seaports. Belloc introduces this twist in the tale when he states:

> upon this original trajectory two exceptions fell in a time so remote that it has hardly left a record. The western end of the road was deflected and came to spring, not from Stonehenge, but from the site of Winchester; the eastern portion was cut short: it terminated, not at some port, but at Canterbury, inland.[46]

Similarly, Belloc argues that Winchester developed a special character, for reasons not unlike Canterbury. Such reasons stemmed from Winchester's location at the end of the Itchen Valley, a continuation of what Belloc describes as the submerged Valley of Southampton Water and in easy reach of the Channel refuges found around the Solent and the Wight. These he includes as: Yarmouth, Lymington, New Town, the Medina, Portsmouth and the Hamble. For early

9 St Martha's chapel, near Guildford on the Pilgrims' Way

sea voyagers, Belloc argues that these were the coastal towns of the Second Crossing that linked Cherbourg on the French coast with the Solent and Southampton Water. He sums up his theory when he states:

It is the perfect harbour, and though it has but lately recovered its ancient importance, the inland waters, known as the Solent, Southampton Water, and Spithead were certainly the chief landing places of these islands. Porchester, Brading, Cowes perhaps, and Bitten certainly, show what the Romans made of the opportunity.[47]

Dr G.B. Grundy, whose work was noted by Ivan Margary, also held the view that the North Downs trackway terminated at Canterbury, which therefore remained consistent with Belloc's theory. It should be remembered that both Margary and Grundy were also looking at the trackway from the perspective of a prehistoric route, although, unlike Grundy, Margary certainly did not hold the view that the trackway diverted to Canterbury rather than maintaining a course along the edge of the Downs to the Straits. For Margary, the route he describes is 'conditioned entirely by local features of geology and geography' and not from the perspective of many earlier writers, of which he says were 'interested in the medieval use of the road'. Here Margary is no doubt alluding to the pilgrimist tradition, but upon referring to Grundy's work he states: 'He appreciated the dual nature of the route, as a ridgeway and a terrace-way, but regarded Canterbury as its natural termination, which, I think wrong, for the route is clearly leading to the Channel coast, as it is hoped now to show.'[48]

But a century earlier and prior to the publication of Allen's essays or the work of Cartwright and Belloc, Dean Stanley in *Historical Memorials of Canterbury*, first published in 1855, had set out the basis for the Pilgrims' Way story. Furthermore, Dean Stanley had made reference not only to the trackway's use by prehistoric travellers, but also linked the road directly with medieval pilgrimage, when he wrote:

> Another line of approach is along the old British track which led across the Surrey downs from Southampton; it can be traced under the name of the Pilgrim's-way or the Pilgrim's lane, marked often by the venerable yews, – usually creeping half-way up the hills immediately above the line of cultivation, and under the highest crest, – passing here and there a solitary chapel or friendly monastery, but avoiding for the most part the towns and villages and regular roads, probably for the same reason as in the days of Shagar, the son of Anath, the highways were unoccupied, and the travellers walked through the byways.[49]

Having developed arguments for a continuous trackway between Winchester and Canterbury, it was then the task of the pilgrimists to establish that their route had ever been trodden by the feet of medieval pilgrims.

2

Towards a Pilgrims' Way Theory

Beyond Cartwright and Belloc

The view that the North Downs trackways also formed part of a continuous route used by medieval pilgrims owes much to a far greater number of people than just Hilaire Belloc and, of course, Julia Cartwright before him. From the late eighteenth century onwards, there have been writers and cartographers who contributed to the development of both the history and the myths associated with the trackway. Nevertheless, any reappraisal of the evidence needs to proceed with caution for, when it comes to the history of ancient trackways, there are ample warnings with regard to the many pitfalls that may befall such a reassessment. For as Christopher Taylor, one of Britain's leading field archaeologists, warns: 'there have appeared many "popular" books on ancient trackways, most of which are largely nonsense and have little or no relevance to the truth.'[1]

Nevertheless, there were elements of the Pilgrims' Way story that received positive criticism from well-respected quarters. We have already seen, for instance, that Ivan Margary held the view that the Pilgrims' Way had special importance and merited more attention than it had been given. However, he did conclude with the caveat that the evidence of the trackway's use by medieval pilgrims is 'admittedly of a negative character'.[2] Notwithstanding this, the extent of its importance led him to suggest that it required a detailed independent survey rather than being left on record as an offshoot of one of the many trackways of Hampshire.

Moreover, Margary also offered an olive branch toward pilgrimist notions when he alluded to the unexplained structural alterations made to St Catherine's Chapel. Interestingly, he refers to an account made by Thackeray Turner in 1890 of St Catherine's Chapel, which lies just to the south of

Guildford. Turner's account identified a peculiar arrangement whereby the upper windows of the chapel had been blocked and had doors inserted to give access to what he believed had been a gallery. Turner also noticed that the doorstops had been designed so that the south door would open inwards and the north door would open outwards, which he believed might be to facilitate 'the passage of large numbers of people through the gallery from north to south'.[3] Therefore, despite Margary's scepticism, he is far from dismissive of the Pilgrims' Way tradition when he concludes that:

> The whole arrangement clearly suggests provision for the handling of visitors in large numbers, and, although an annual fair was customarily held there, this in itself seems inadequate to account for so remarkable a building. Parties of devout people visiting it frequently seem necessary to explain it, and thus the battered little building may retain vital evidence in support of the pilgrim tradition.[4]

We have seen how, as late as the 1960s, commentators such as Timperley and Brill in *Ancient Trackways of Wessex* and Cochrane in *The Lost Roads of Wessex* were referring to the Pilgrims' Way as a continuation of the trackway from Hampshire known as the Harroway and, as such, the Pilgrims' Way's acceptance as a prehistoric trackway was fairly secure. We've also examined how Belloc turned the ancient trackway's east–west axis on its head, developing an argument for the way's evolution from migration route to trade route. Consequential to this was also the necessity for the southern hub towns of Canterbury and Winchester, which were equidistant and within easy reach of their respective satellite port towns. For Belloc these hub towns were certainly pre-Roman, for as he states:

> Of both towns we are certain that they were prehistoric centres. Not only have the earliest implements of men been discovered in their soil, but it is evident that the prehistoric mode of defence in these islands was used by each – a camp or temporary refuge crowning a hill above the settlement and defended by great circumvallations of earth. Canterbury has the Iron Age camp in Bigberry Wood; Winchester has that upon St. Catherine's Hill. In each town a considerable British population existed before the Roman invasion.[5]

At the Canterbury end of the Pilgrims' Way, the predominant view is that the Iron Age settlement was at Bigbury Camp, previously known locally as Bigberry Camp. Situated about a mile and a half to the west of the present city of Canterbury, it probably served as an Iron Age hill fort for the protection of local farmers in periods of danger. The site covers an area of 25 acres and includes a cattle annex or compound, defended by a ditch to the north, and is believed to date from the Iron Age, 800 BC through to AD 42.[6] However, Ashbee suggests that sometime after 54 BC the site was abandoned. A series of archaeological excavations found iron and bronze items, including slave chain neck-rings, horse gear vehicle fittings, cauldron chains, fetters and fire-dogs.[7] The camp is particularly notable because many commentators believe that Bigbury was overrun by the Romans in 54 BC and is the hill fort documented by Julius Caesar in Book V of the *Gallic Wars*. Interestingly though, there is very little evidence of there ever having been a Roman presence at Bigbury. However a LiDAR survey of Blean Woods, which pulses lasers from a plane to reveal hidden features obscured by woodland, has shown further extensive earthworks to the north of Bigbury Camp and very close to the likely line of Watling Street.[8] This site may yet provide evidence that supports not only British occupation but also archaeological evidence linking it to the Roman 7th Legion.

So Belloc paints a picture for his readers whereby, around the end of the twelfth century, medieval pilgrims are passing Bigbury just before entering the walls of Canterbury. In true pilgrimist tradition, both Belloc and Cartwright claim the Pilgrims' Way as passing through Bigbury Camp. Yet in 1893 Cartwright merely suggested that 'the Pilgrims' Way descends into the valley of the Stour, and after following the course of the river for a short time, climbs the opposite hill and strikes into Bigberry Wood'.[9] However eighteen years later, by the time of the third reprint of Julia Cartwright's *Pilgrims' Way from Winchester to Canterbury*, the work had been considerably revised. In the revised edition Cartwright acknowledges the work of H. Snowden-Ward's *The Canterbury Pilgrimages*, as well as the work of Elliston-Erwood, who had at that time yet to express doubts about the veracity of the Way as a pilgrimage route.

It is a reflection of the development of the Pilgrims' Way narrative that Cartwright recognised how within the twenty years of her original publication 'a whole literature had grown up around the Pilgrims' Way'.[10] And Cartwright herself is reinforcing her own account of the Pilgrims' Way and its links with the camp through drawing from the works of other pilgrimist writers. Not only does Cartwright link Bigbury Camp with the Pilgrims' Way, but she also combines the two by reference to popular folklore, when she informs her readers how the Pilgrims' Way comes to the:

> fort which the Britons held against the assault of the Roman invaders, and which was stormed and carried by Caesar's legions. The memory of that desperate fight, which sealed the fate of Britain and her conquest by the great Proconsul, still lingers in the popular mind, and the shepherd who

follows his flock and the waggoner who drives his team along the road, still
talk of this famous battle two thousand years ago.[11]

Belloc's view that Canterbury supplanted Dover at the eastern end of the
ancient trackway, with Winchester supplanting Stonehenge at the western
end, was not completely new. Dr Grundy's view that a North Downs trackway terminated at Canterbury remained consistent with that espoused by
Albert Way in his essay 'The Pilgrims' Way or path towards the Shrine of St
Thomas of Canterbury', which provides much of the narrative for Belloc's
subsequent work that was to be published nearly a half century later. Albert
Way offered not only Winchester and Canterbury, but a route very close to
the one later described by both Belloc and Cartwright.

From Pre-historic Trackway to Pilgrimage Route

As we have seen, before the turn of the nineteenth century fascination with
the pilgrims' route had also caught the imagination of a woman, renowned as a
historian and art critic of the Italian Renaissance. Mrs Ady's book, *The Pilgrims
Way – from Winchester to Canterbury*,[12] written under her maiden name Julia
Cartwright, was published eleven years prior to the publication of Belloc's
The Old Road. Nevertheless, whereas Belloc undertook the journey on foot
between Winchester and Canterbury, it is doubtful that Mrs Ady actually
walked any great distance of her subject matter.[13] More importantly, Belloc
was the first writer to attempt an overall theory about the history, origins and
survival of a trackway connecting Winchester with Canterbury, which up until
then had been a piecemeal process undertaken by local antiquarians.

It has also been suggested that, in the eight days Belloc allowed himself
to survey the route, given the time of year he chose to undertake the task,
it would have been difficult for him to cover the whole length. Even today,
with much of the Way well maintained and incorporated into long-distance
footpaths, eight days would present a challenging time schedule. Apparently
Belloc commenced his survey of the Pilgrims' Way on 22 December 1899,
with the aim of completion on 29 December, so as to arrive at Canterbury
on the anniversary of the martyrdom. Sean Jennett observed that, taking
account of the time of year, this would have given Belloc 56 hours of day-
light to cover 112 miles, or 14 miles day – a schedule that Jennett doubts
Belloc could have achieved.[14]

Although Belloc offered an all-embracing theory of the 'old road', he
too, like Cartwright, acknowledged his debt to other antiquarians. He had
undoubtedly built upon the previous work of Albert Way, who many com-

mentators on the Pilgrims' Way either overlook or infer that he reached over-enthusiastic conclusions regarding his theories about the trackway. Furthermore, Albert Way is fairly instrumental in terms of the notion that pilgrims used it as a route to Canterbury. In fact, as C.G. Crump notes, with a slight hint of cynicism, in an essay entitled 'The Pilgrims Way', 'up until 1850 the Pilgrims' Road has made no progress eastward since the early years of the century ... It had never crossed the Medway'[15] – that was until Albert Way developed a theory of the Way following 'the ancient British tracks that crossed the valley to the Wye and went by Stowting to the coast'.[16] Despite the drubbing some later commentators gave Albert Way, the British Museum recognises his contribution as an important nineteenth-century antiquarian. Moreover, it has been suggested that this is reflected in Way's correspondence with A.F. Franks, which demonstrates his contribution towards a local archaeological tradition and the establishment of national and regional archaeological museum collections.[17]

The reality was that Albert Way's theory of the 'Way or path towards the shrine of Thomas of Canterbury' had a flaw, in as much as he couldn't get his pilgrims to Canterbury. In fact, he could only get them as far as the point where the River Stour cuts a path through the chalk downs on its course due north-east to Canterbury and the sea. Albert Way needed to get his medieval travellers off what he described as the ancient British track and head due north-east along the Stour Valley to Canterbury. And it is at Wye that Way is helped by a hypothesis presented to him by Rev. W. Pearson, who states 'that an ancient track, still known as the Pilgrims Road, exists, running above the Ashford and Canterbury turnpike road and parallel with it'.[18]

An antiquarian who devoted a great deal of study to the Pilgrims' Way and was recognised by Ivan Margary for his work on the Surrey section was Dr Edwin Hart, whose collection of work and extensive collection of photographic glass slides are held by the Guildford Museum.[19] Hart was passionate about the Pilgrims' Way and in an article published in *Surrey Archaeological Collections* he argued that criticisms of the 'Old Way', such as those raised by Elliston-Erwood and H.W. Knocker, were 'largely due to neglect of existing records and lack of close acquaintance with the line of the road'.[20] Nevertheless, Hart did argue 'that the Old Way really began at the sea ports of East Kent' and, as such, was building upon the foundations laid by earlier writers with regard to the prehistoric route. Moreover, Hart argued that the original route from the Kent coast remained 'in existence right across the county as late as 1769'.

In Surrey and Kent there was an alternative route south of the Pilgrims' Way, which went along the lower greensand through Dorking, Reigate, Westerham and Maidstone. Nevertheless, it was Hart's view that the older route in both winter and summer offered fast foot and horse traffic a superior route 'owing to the wear and tear of the heavier wheeled traffic through the villages and utter lack of any system of road repair'.[21]

Characteristics of the Trackway

What then were the characteristics of the Pilgrims' Way that may have offered medieval travellers a superior route? An important factor, when this is considered, along with its use as a principal thoroughfare across Kent and Surrey and on into Hampshire, is that to its south the road network was often non-existent. It has been noted by Peter Brandon in his study *The Kent and Sussex Weald* that as late as the eighteenth century the Weald was roadless.[22] Brandon notes how J.A. Malcolm, writing as late as the eighteenth century, described at the time the difficult conditions that were encountered travelling in the Low Weald when he 'had to find a guide to take him from Ockley to Rudgwick. Although only 30 miles from London, the distance of six miles took him four hours with good horses.'[23]

The communities in the Weald remained effectively isolated and had to wait for the turnpike roads of the eighteenth century before they were able to overcome a lack of communication links, which Brandon describes as having a major detrimental impact on the development of the Wealden economy. The example of Ockley is particularly relevant because the village is situated close to Dorking and only 6 miles south of the Pilgrims' Way and the chalk escarpment, where the geological characteristics of the escarpment offered far more appealing conditions for travellers underfoot.

Norbert Ohler's study of travel in the Middle Ages captures the likely condition of roads that the medieval traveller experienced. In Ohler's book, *The Medieval Traveller*, he argues that despite the condition of many trackways, these routes had some advantages over the Roman roads, particularly for horses and pack-animals. Describing the state of the roads, he says:

> Even the roads called 'street' were generally only about four or five metres wide, so two vehicles might meet in the middle. Proper maintenance of roads was not carried out in Europe – with few exceptions – until the end of the eighteenth or the beginning of the nineteenth century; until then pot-holes were filled in with earth and brushwood when necessary. Such roads had some advantages over the paved Roman roads: they were less susceptible to frost, easy to repair and provided a better surface for horse and pack animals which were shod.[24]

10 London Lane, Holloway, linking Shere and the Pilgrims' Way

11 Lenham Cross war memorial, cut into the chalk escarpment, Pilgrims' Way

12 St Benedict's pilgrims' chapel, Paddlesworth

The Pilgrims' Way has been described as both a ridge walk and a terrace-way. For identification purposes a good rule of thumb is that the old trackway kept to the lower southern slopes because these were less exposed than the upper ridge. Where it does follow the ridge, the Way often sits a little lower than the crest, seeking shelter just below the southern side of the ridge. However, the road is most frequently found just above the woods of the Weald or the cultivated land of the vale at the foot of the escarpment, avoiding the claggy clay found on the lower ground. Today, if one walks along the North Downs Way National Trail, it can be seen that sections of the trail signposted as the 'Pilgrims' Way' are often just a few metres above the fields at the foot of the North Downs escarpment, but high enough to benefit from the better drainage of the chalk and flint soil. Ivan Margary is of the opinion that:

> it is probable that the earliest trackway followed the crest, at a time when security of look out was more vital than the avoidance of wet feet, but that eventually the terrace-way route, avoiding the sticky summit and keeping

upon the clean Chalk near the foot, was formed also. This has to keep close in to the foot of the range because another sticky stratum, the Gault Clay, lies parallel with it just below the Chalk, forming a very wet belt of land in the vale below.[25]

Today there are many places where sections of ancient terrace-way can still be seen as well as explored on foot. For instance, at Paddlesworth, just west of the Medway Gap, a large section of ancient trackway, some of which has not been incorporated into the North Downs Way National Trail, can clearly be seen. The track runs about 2 metres above the field system and passes within 500 metres of St Benedictine's church, which is 900 years old. The Churches Conservation Trust suggests in its history of St Benedict's that many medieval pilgrims left the trail and stopped to pray on their way to Becket's shrine. Again at Dunn Street, west of Westwell, the terrace-way is still clearly seen just above the field system and long sections between Wye and Postling above Brabourne exhibit the characteristics of terrace-way. This section is still used as a public road and known as the Pilgrims' Way.

3

Cartographers and the Pilgrims' Way

Cartographers and the Trackway

Fundamental to any debate about the Pilgrims' Way is the search for evidence of the trackway's depiction in early attempts to incorporate roads on maps of southern England. Amongst the earliest maps to include roads are the four drawn by Matthew Paris, a monk at St Albans abbey, in 1250. Paris' maps show a route via Canterbury, Rochester and then on to London and, as such, offer no direct evidence with regard to the existence of the Pilgrims' Way.

Just over a hundred years later the Gough map, estimated to have been drawn around 1360 and named after the eighteenth-century antiquarian Richard Gough, includes a total of 2940 miles of roads across England. Roads are denoted by a thin red line connecting towns on the map, which shows a route from Winchester to London via Guildford, which could align with towns along the Pilgrims' Way between Alresford and Guildford. But after Guildford, the route depicted on the Gough map continues via Cobham and Kingston then on to London. It should be noted that there is no route shown from London due east into Kent and, as such, omits the Kent section of Watling Street. Notwithstanding this, the Gough map does highlight towns to the east of Guildford, such as Dorking and Reigate, that are close to the Pilgrims' Way, and similar to the towns on the line of a known route like Watling Street are not shown as connected by a red line. Therefore, absence of a red route on the Gough map is not necessarily evidence that a road did not exist.

Interestingly, the only route through Kent depicted by the Gough map's red lines is the route that ran between Southampton and Canterbury. This route is shown as passing through Sussex, then north towards Canterbury

13 Reputed grave of Richard Plantagenet, son of Richard III, St Mary's Church, Eastwell

from Rye and, as such, is of no relevance to the route of the Pilgrims' Way. This is discussed in greater detail below.

By 1596, Philip Symonson of Rochester had produced a half-inch map, *A New Description of Kent*, which showed a number of roads radiating from Canterbury. However, the route to Canterbury closest to the Pilgrims' Way leaves the chalk escarpment and crosses the Downs, passing just west of Challock, rather than staying with the chalk escarpment and meeting the Stour Valley at Eastwell or Boughton Aluph before turning north-east towards Canterbury, as does the Pilgrims' Way. The route shown on Symonson's map also crosses the Stour at a ford just before Chartham and enters Canterbury from the south rather than the west of the city. A comparison of the two routes is shown in the diagram below.

From Charing, Symonson's road westward appears to stay lower in the vale than the Pilgrims' Way and passes just to the south of Lenham, whereas the Pilgrims' Way maintains the higher ground north of Lenham. This pattern continues with Symonson's road through the vale, keeping to the lower

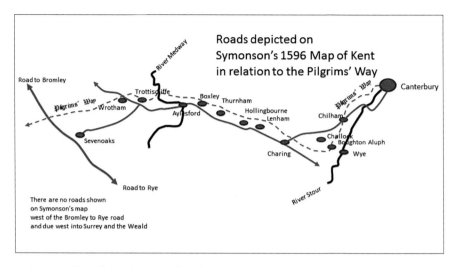

14 Symonson's roads in relation to the Pilgrims' Way

ground, well to the south of Hollingbourne and Thurnham, until it crosses the River Medway at Aylesford. After Trottiscliffe, any vague similarity with the route taken by the Pilgrims' Way certainly ends, because from here Symonson shows one road going in a north-westerly direction to Kingsdowne and another going in a south-westerly direction to Sevenoaks. From Trottiscliffe there is no road shown as heading directly west and no road whatsoever shown as running into Surrey and west of the Bromley to Rye Road.

In 2010 work being undertaken by South East Water at Bearsted, near Maidstone, uncovered what archaeologists described as the impressive remains of a Roman road. One theory postulated is that this road linked Maidstone with Faversham. If this were so, then it would add to our understanding of travel through the Vale of Holmesdale east of Maidstone and in particular how we assess through-routes such as the Pilgrims' Way.

In 1801 Faden published the first map of the county of Kent, surveyed by the Ordnance Survey and published for general use in the scale of 1 inch to 1 mile. The survey was undertaken by Captain William Mudge of the Royal Artillery. The trackways and roads that have become known as the Pilgrims' Way were clearly depicted on the map, as can be seen from the illustration below. Edwin Hart noted that, with the exception of two breaks at Chevening and Titsey Park, a continuous route of what he termed the 'Old Way' could be located on the 1801 and 1819 1-inch ordnance sheets:

> Now we find, both on the ground and on old maps, that a line of the old
> road can be traced westwards from Eastwell Park for long stretches invari-
> ably in the same position, just below the steep southern slope of the upper

chalk; always in the same alignment, with no immediately apparent destination, and very rarely passing through a village, through connected with
many by short branch roads. The modern maps show certain breaks in the
line, but if we examine the early Kent and Surrey Ordnance sheets of 1801
and 1819 on the 1" scale we find that no breaks then existed, except two
across the park of Chevening and Titsey.[1]

West of Titsey Park, Hart recognised that tracing the Pilgrims' Way became
more difficult and remarked 'that if the road did go farther it had largely
disappeared before 1764, or was then so little used that it was not shown by
Rocque, on his map of that date'.[2] Hart undertook his own survey of the
route west of Titsey and came to the conclusion after extensive field surveys
and evidence from numerous sources. These sources included Rocque's map
of Surrey, 1764; tithe maps of Catherham, Chaldon, Buckland and Blechingly;
Lord Hylton's estate map of Gatton, Mertsham and Chaldon; Budgen's field
map of Netley Farm, 1724, as well as evidence contained in a number of road-
closing orders. Hart's conclusion was that a continuous line for the road could
be traced right through to the Shalford ferry-crossing just south of Guildford.

Hart's view was that the fact the Saxon villages were not situated on the line
of the Pilgrims' Way but to the south of it suggested that the way was already
developed prior to the establishment of the villages. The Saxon farmsteads,
he argued, were developed to the south of the way, near to sources of water.
Between Gatton and Eastwell the only two villages settled in Roman times
were Otford and Titsey, and these both had sources of water, whereas there
are a further 20 Saxon villages to be found just to the south of the Pilgrims'

15 OS map surveyed by Captain Mudge 1801 (reproduced with kind permission of the
Centre for Kentish Studies)

16 St Swithun's Saxon church, Headbourne Worthy

Way. His conclusion was that the Pilgrims' Way was a 'definite through route of pre-Saxon date'.[3]

Of course, archaeology is continually revealing new clues about our past and recent excavations in Kent at the White Horse Stone junction of the Pilgrims' Way and the Roman road that ran from Rochester to Hastings were undertaken as part of the Channel Tunnel Rail Link project. The excavations showed the Pilgrims' Way to be of at least middle Anglo-Saxon date.[4]

Andrew Reynolds, writing about the archaeology of the Channel Tunnel Rail Link, described the findings as follows:

> The large scale investigations at White Horse Stone have provided a valuable archaeological view of the intersection between a major Roman route, leading south from Rochester across the Weald towards Hastings and the so-called Pilgrims Way, a late name given to an early route, perhaps even that used by William during his conquest of Kent immediately following Hastings and on his (rather circuitous) way to London (Banyard 2004, 34). Archaeology shows that the route is indeed ancient.[5]

The excavations revealed three holloways, all of which were described as having flint metalling. The earliest of these had a slightly different alignment to the later holloways. The latter two aligned with the course of the present Pilgrims' Way. Reynolds suggests that the three routes reflect how early roads would often detour in periods of wet weather when one stretch became impassable.

As well as the three holloways, the site also revealed the body of an Anglo-Saxon woman that had been buried at the crossroads.

Reynolds suggests that the reason the woman was buried at the crossroads may have been to permanently remove her from the realm of the living and prevent her ghost from returning to the community. Such burials may have been associated with outcasts, outsiders or those who committed suicide. As such, the burial find at the crossroads suggests that the Pilgrims' Way was considered beyond or on the edge of the local community and served as a through-route. The dating of the road and its relationship with the community supports many of the views of Edwin Hart that we have already considered.

The Trackway and Pilgrimage

But what of the pilgrims who are believed to have adopted the ancient terrace-ways and ridge tracks, from whom this ancient trackway takes its name? Medieval pilgrimage to the shrine of Thomas Becket followed the archbishop's murder in 1170 and continued until the destruction of the shrine during the Reformation – a period that spanned 368 years. But history moves on and it is interesting that during the course of the last three centuries the use of the Pilgrims' Way has become a route of revived pilgrimage. Irrespective of the how one interprets the Way's previous history, people undertake pilgrimage along it today because they bring to it their own understanding of what the trackway's history is.

However, both the period of medieval pilgrimage, as well as that of any later revival, is a relatively short period in the overall history of the North Downs' trackways, but an important period nonetheless for those with an eye to the pilgrimist tradition. Only through an appreciation of the trackway's broader story can we begin to gain an insight into those who may have used it; why they may have used it; and the trackway's place in a changing landscape, and then we can begin to assess it within the context of the medieval traveller.

Exactly how well does pilgrimage fit with the ancient trackway? Some commentators like Hilaire Belloc and Julia Cartwright have suggested that pilgrimage saved the 'old road' as its use started to decline. Belloc's view was that by the time of Becket's death, Winchester's importance had started to diminish as London grew in importance and became the new base for the English monarchs. Moreover, his theory is that the very trade that had sustained the use of the prehistoric trackway declined as fewer metals were coming up from the West Country as the Sussex iron industry in the Weald had taken their place. No longer was an extended route to the west of the country of such primary importance.

17 Scallop carving on Christ
Church Gate, Canterbury

Published records of gifts and offerings made at the cathedral between 1207
and 1532 suggest that in the jubilee year of 1420 over 100,000 people may
have visited the shrine. Elliston-Erwood noted from the recorded offerings
that another high point was in 1220, the first jubilee year, and suggests that 'on
the basis of the 1420 offerings (bearing in mind the change of money value),
about a quarter of a million people visited the Shrine – a rather incredible
number'.[6] Furthermore, the Paston letters suggest that even more pilgrims
visited Canterbury in 1471. In a letter to his son, Sir John Paston wrote on 28
September 1471 that: 'As ffor tydyngs, the Kyng and the Qwywn and moche
other pepall ar ryden and goon to Canterbery. Nevyr so moche peple seyn in
Pylgrymage hertofor at ones, as men sayd.'[7] The extent to which analysis of
offerings can provide clues of the scale of medieval pilgrimage is examined in
greater detail in Chapter 7.

Sean Sennett in his book *The Pilgrims Way – from Winchester to Canterbury*
reminds the reader that 'the Way must have been the route taken by Henry
II in July 1174, when he landed at Southampton and rode eastwards to make
his belated but massive and painful penance at Canterbury'.[8] No documentary evidence has been found that can clearly pinpoint the exact route

Henry II took. But it is known that Henry II stopped at Harbledown village with its Chaucerian associations. It is the view of many commentators that Harbledown is the village referred to as 'Bob-up-and-down' by Chaucer in the Manciple's prologue, for it says:

> Wite ye nat wher ther stant a little toun
> Which that y-cleped is Bob-up-and-down
> Under the Blee, in Caunterbury Waye

From Harbledown, Henry II dismounted from his horse and commenced the final mile and a half of his journey barefoot, after stopping to pray in the church of St Nicholas, which belonged to the leper hospital established by Archbishop Lanfranc in 1084. Nestling just below the hospital of St Nicholas is to be found the Black Prince's Well, where the Black Prince is supposed to have stopped and drunk from the lepers' well on his way to Canterbury in 1357.

Chaucer's Pilgrims and the Pilgrims' Way

A common misconception is that there is a link between Chaucer's pilgrims and the route of the Pilgrims' Way. So what of Chaucer's fictional pilgrims, whose journey to Canterbury led them along what was most likely the Roman road we now call Watling Street?[9] Tracing the Chaucerian route to Canterbury owes much to the work of Henry Littlehales, whose *Some Notes on the Road from London to Canterbury in the Middle Ages* was published in 1898. A useful summary of Littlehales' work is to be found in Jack Ravensdale's book *In the Steps of Chaucer's Pilgrims*. Ravensdale makes a very important distinction between the Pilgrims' Way and Chaucer's London to Canterbury route when he notes that:

> A strange feature appears from examining the whole length of the route from London to Canterbury and beyond on the early editions of the Ordnance Survey. Whereas long stretches of prehistoric trackway on the roads from Canterbury to Dover and Southampton are called the Pilgrims' Way, the nearest that the road from Canterbury to London gets such an appellation is a very short length on the final approach to the City, which is called the Pilgrims' Road.[10]

This final stretch on the approach to Canterbury called the Pilgrims' Road is where the Chaucerian route may have converged with the Winchester route in the mile or so between the village of Harbledown and Canterbury. Today,

Chaucer's Watling Street from London is fairly unsightly and a busy route for traffic for much of its length. It follows the modern A2 and even in Kent it is caught in the sprawl of the Medway conurbation, which extends through Strood, Chatham, Gillingham and Rainham. The road then passes through a succession of towns before reaching Faversham and Boughton-under-Blean, before climbing over the forest of the Blean to reach Canterbury. As Ravensdale points out, it is worth noting that Littlehales 'slips into heading his map of the whole road from London to Canterbury, The Pilgrims' Way' and goes on to suggest that 'For us the pilgrims' way par excellence is the route from Southwark to Canterbury, and approaching the landscape through Chaucer studies we tend, unwittingly, to hi-jack in our minds the name of other prehistoric tracks for Watling Street and its subsidiaries'.[11]

For those walking the Pilgrims' Way who choose to follow the St Swithun's Way from Winchester to Farnham, then the North Downs Way National Trail from Farnham through to Canterbury, the only occasions that the journey coincides with Chaucer's route is at Rochester and then again after Blean Woods at Harbledown village. For purists following likely Pilgrims' Way routes, thereby crossing the River Medway further upstream, at Snodland, Halling or Aylesford, then Rochester would be bypassed as well.[12] But whilst there is little association of Chaucer's route with the Pilgrims' Way, there is evidence to link the denotation of 'pilgrim' with the North Downs trackway. Moreover, much of this evidence predates Cartwright and Belloc.

Use of the Name 'Pilgrims' Way'

Many commentators have suggested that the first recorded evidence of the North Downs trackways being referred to as the Pilgrims' Road dates from when an Ordnance Survey officer, Captain E. Renouard James, designated parts of the trackway on the first edition 6-inch maps of Kent and Surrey, which were prepared between 1861 and 1871. Wilfrid Hooper states that James had a keen interest in archaeology and was elected to the Council of the Society in 1888. He was keen to remind readers in an article for the *Surrey Archaeological Collections* that James had opened his notes of 1871 'with the damaging confession that the subject of the Pilgrims' Way had been little studied in west Surrey and that "very many persons" in that neighbourhood "were in ignorance of the very name"'.[13]

However, both Hasted's map-maker, in his map of the Codsheath Hundred in 1778–79, and the Andrews, Dury and Herbert 2-inch Kent map of 1769 mark sections of road under the Downs as the Pilgrim Road.

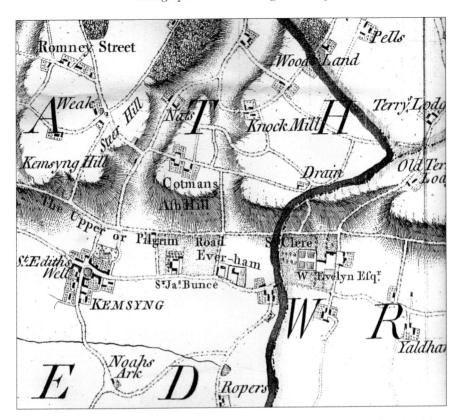

18 Andrews, Dury and Herbert 1769, showing Pilgrim Road at Kemsing (reproduced with kind permission of the Centre for Kentish Studies)

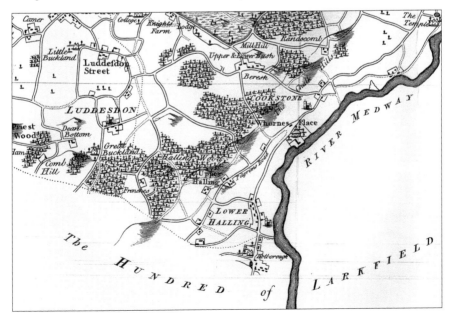

19 Hasted 1797, 2nd edition, showing Pilgrims Road at Lower Halling

The Andrews, Dury and Herbert map of 1769 shows the Pilgrim Road at the foot of the escarpment just above Kemsing. The current Ordnance Survey 1:25000 series (4cm to 1km) marks the road in an identical position and denotes it as 'Pilgrims' Way Trackway', with trackway shown in an Old English typeface. Hasted's *History of Kent*, published between 1778 and 1799, includes a map of the Codsheath Hundred that marks the Pilgrims' Road as it is also shown on the earlier Andrews, Dury and Herbert map referred to above.

Hasted's map of the Hundreds of Toltingtrough and Shamel also shows the Pilgrims' Road marked on the escarpment road on the west bank of the Medway Valley, just west of Lower Halling. Although this is clearly a continuation of the lower trackway below the Birling ridge, the track is marked at a point close to Lower Halling, which is past Belloc's favoured crossing point at Snodland. As such, many of Belloc's travellers would have struck out into the valley, having left the trackway a mile or so before reaching Lower Halling. This begs the question as to why the Pilgrims' Road continued north-east along the side of the Medway Valley towards Rochester if the majority of travellers coming from the west crossed the Medway further upstream. A fuller discussion of this point can be found in Chapter 6.

What is important is that, 100 years before Captain James included the appellation 'Pilgrims' Road' on the first edition of the 6-inch Ordnance Survey maps, other cartographers had already used the appellation on some sections of the road.

The Kemsing Milestone

A milestone dating from early eighteenth century can still be found at the north side of the junction of the Pilgrims' Way with the road to Seal, known as Child's Bridge Road at TQ 547592. It is of particular interest for two reasons. The first reason is that the milestone is situated on the Pilgrims' Road and predates the toll road. The second is that the inscription on the west face of the stone is 'to Malling 10 miles'. Elliston-Erwood described the stone in 'Miscellaneous Notes on some Kent roads' in 1956. He suggested that of greater importance than the age of the stone, which he suggested might be the earliest dated milestone (other than those of Roman origin), is what it tells us about road system prior to the turnpike. As he states:

> But of greater importance than the stone are the roads it indicates, for here we
> have a part of the road system that preceded the introduction of the Turnpike,
> and included in this scheme is a section of the 'Pilgrims' Road' that has hith-
> erto not been regarded as anything but a country track or at most a by-road.[14]

20 Milestone on the Pilgrims' Way at Kemsing

Furthermore, Elliston-Erwood argues the milestone is significant because it offers 'undisputable proof' that at the end of the seventeenth century, between Otford and Wrotham, the Pilgrims' Road was in use as a highway.

The West Kent Tithe Case

Research undertaken by Capt. H.W. Knocker found that in all West Kent parish tithe apportionments that 'woodlands south of the Pilgrims Road pay no tithe'.[15] Elliston-Erwood argues that 'evidently in Kent there was a well-recognised continuous track on the chalk hills, and that later this was known as the Pilgrim's Road'. Robert Furley's two-volume study, *A History of the Weald of Kent*, published 1871–74, looks at the boundary of the Weald and devotes a number of pages to what became known as the West Kent Tithe Case, tried at Croydon before Lord Ellenborough and a special jury on 28 July 1815. Furley's account of the case is taken from the shorthand writer's report of the case printed by Wickham and Cutbush in 1815. It is noteworthy in respect of the Pilgrims' Way because the outcome of the case depended upon whether or not the Pilgrims' Road constituted the boundary of the Weald or forest of Kent. The council for Lord Le Despenser, the plaintiff, contended that:

the Weald of Kent is bounded on the north by the Chalk and not the Red
Hills; that at the Bottom of these chalk hills there is an ancient lane or road
called the Pilgrims' Road, and that whatever lies above it to the north is out
of the Weald of Kent, and whatever lies to the south of this road is within
it; that the land in dispute formed part of a large district of woodland, {the
greater part of which has been grubbed up}, known as the Blaize and called
the Hurst Woods, which was within the Weald; that the Pilgrims' Road was
not only the boundary of the Weald in Aylesford, but in other adjoining
parishes; that all the woods within the Weald were by immemorial custom
exempt from the payment of tithe; and that there is another custom in the
Weald called land peerage, by which all timber growing on waste land, and
the outrunnings of woods and fields, belong to the owner of the adjoining
land, and not the to the Lord of the Manor.[16]

One witness, Mr John Ward of Westerham, stated that the 'Pilgrims' Road
ran immediately under the white hills' and that he had heard 'his father and
other witnesses say, he considered the Pilgrims' Road was the boundary'. More
importantly, Mr Ward also gave evidence that about twenty years previously
'he was requested with his brother magistrates to decide whether it would be
detrimental to the public if the road in question was diverted'. Furley adds this
date in brackets in his account of proceedings and judges it to have been 1793.[17]

In the whole of Furley's account of the West Kent Tithe Case, in which he
cites at length from Sir Samuel Shepherd the Solicitor-General's reply on behalf
of Lord Le Despencer, as well as from evidence for the defendant given by
Sergeant Best (later Lord Wynford), there is no question about the validity of the
Pilgrims' Road. Neither side question the use of the name, and it appears that
this was generally accepted. It is only whether or not the Pilgrims' Road was
the accepted boundary of the Weald that was in doubt. The case implies that,
at least from the testimony of witnesses from the Kent border at Westerham,
through Chevening and even past Boxley on the east side of the Medway, there
was widespread acknowledgement that the lane below the chalk was known
as the Pilgrims' Road as far back as the middle of the eighteenth century. The
fact that Earl Stanhope claimed that 'he had always understood from his father
and the old inhabitants' that the Pilgrims' Road was the boundary of the Weald
would appear to push the date back at least into the 1700s.[18]

Furley's first volume of *The History of the Weald* also mentions the West Kent
Tithe Case and makes reference to the boundary of the Weald in connection
with the Pilgrims' Way. Here Furley uses the words 'groundless' and 'erroneously', but it is obvious upon closer reading that Furley is referring to the
tradition of the Pilgrims' Way serving as the boundary of the Weald being
groundless rather than the use of the pathway by pilgrims.

One of the many pilgrims' pathways to Canterbury led from Hampshire over the Forest ridge in the direction of Canterbury; and when it entered Kent gave rise to a groundless tradition that this pilgrims' way formed the boundary of the Weald of Kent. That the pilgrims would travel on the out-skirts of the Forest was more than probable, and the way they so tracked out might naturally, though erroneously, lead to such a conclusion.[19]

Furley is a good example of a writer making reference to the Pilgrims' Way story prior to Cartwright or Belloc, and perhaps more importantly, push-ing the date of evidence of the use of the appellation Pilgrims' Way, Road or Lane back long before Captain E. Renouard James undertook his survey work for the Ordnance Survey for their first in-house maps in the 1860 and 1870s. Certainly within much of the literature about the Pilgrims' Way's pedi-gree, the date of the mapping undertaken by Captain E.R. James recurs time and again and is seen as a defining event with regard to the name Pilgrims' Way being applied to the trackway. An example of this is the introduction to Curtis and Walker's *Guide to the North Downs Way* which states:

> In fact, many believe that the Pilgrims' Way did not acquire its appella-tion until the 1860s, when an Ordnance Survey officer decided that the route should be so called. Prior to that, local historians have been unable to unearth any such designation.[20]

Captain James, the Ordnance Survey officer in question had his *Notes on the Pilgrims' Way in West Surrey* published for an exhibition held in Shalford Park for the Bath and West of England and Southern Counties Association in May 1871. No doubt one of the reasons he had been invited to contribute towards the exhibition was, as James points out in his notes, because Shalford Park is 'upon the direct line of the ancient road known as the Pilgrims' Way'.[21] Interestingly, James only cites one authority upon which he based his own views of the route taken by the road through Surrey and Kent, and this is Albert Way's appendix to Dean Stanley's *Memorials of Canterbury*. He does, however, place much emphasis on the numerous fairs held close to the Way, which he argues were used by pilgrims en route to Canterbury and that 'the dates upon which these events are fixed are strongly confirmatory of my views as to the fairs being among the results of pilgrimage'.[22] However, James' assertion has come in for a degree of criticism from pilgrimist critics who point to the fact that the time spread of these fairs across the year does not fit neatly with the anniversary of Becket's death on 29 December nor the translation on 7 July and, as such, James' argument suggests pilgrims had an immense amount of time to spend visiting fairs along the route. Shalford fair was held on 14–16 August; Guildford fair on 24 September; and Puttenham fair on 27 June.[23] Elliston-Erwood remarked that to visit these fairs pilgrims must be 'persons with unlimited leisure who spent months on the journey' and points out that James asked his readers 'to believe that the ordinary pilgrim took upwards of a month to perform a journey of 80 miles'.[24]

Despite quoting only one authority in his notes, Captain James does introduce a novel notion of his own. He explains that in the course of his enquiries it had occurred to him that John Bunyan's *Pilgrims' Progress* may depict scenes from the pilgrimage to Canterbury and, referring to Bunyan, informed his readers that:

> In the age in which he lived religious controversy excited every mind; and the Canterbury Pilgrimage being a fresh tradition, does it not give additional interest to the perusal of 'Pilgrims' Progress', if the supposition be permitted that Bunyan selected the worldly and historical Pilgrimage as the basis for his allegory of the life of Christian?[25]

James suggests that similarities can be found between Bunyan's Slough of Despond and the Shalford swamp; the Delectable Mountains and the Surrey Hills; the Hill Difficulty and St Martha's Hill; the Valley of Humiliation and the Vale of Albury; and Vanity Fair and Shalford Fair.

Perhaps it is deeply ironic that Bunyan, who fought for the Parliamentarian side at the siege of Leicester in the English Civil War, narrowly escaped being shot while standing sentry and then was later imprisoned for 12 years after being convicted of preaching as a nonconformist preacher without a licence, may have influenced Captain E.R. James' use of the Pilgrims' Road appellation on the first edition of the Ordnance Survey sheets of Kent and Surrey.[26] Within 200 years of Bunyan's death, his work, which offered an allegory of man's personal journey towards God, may have influenced the inclusion of a route of worldly pilgrimage on Ordnance Survey maps that has continued to the present day. Moreover, a worldly pilgrimage was the very antithesis of what puritans such as Bunyan thought of as the true route to salvation.

Although Captain E.R. James does not mention the work of Manning and Bray in his notes, he must have been aware of their work as they made reference to the Pilgrims' Road in Surrey 63 years before James undertook his survey.

In 1767 the antiquarian Owen Manning asked William Bray, a Surrey-based solicitor from Shere, to help edit his notes for a work on the history of Surrey. Bray was recognised in his own right for his antiquarian work and held the position of Treasurer to the Society of Antiquaries between 1803 and 1823. Manning and Bray's three-volume *The History and Antiquities of the County of Surrey* was researched over 40 years and published between 1804 and 1814.

21 Door to St Lawrence Church, Alton, with pike and musket damage from the English Civil War

22 Detail of damaged door

Surrey County Council state that it is 'still acknowledged as one of the finest county histories of its day'.

Manning and Bray's history refers to two sections of road in Surrey that were known as the Pilgrims' Lane or Road. One length is in Reigate and Merstham, and the other is in Titsey and Tatsfield. According to Manning and Bray the first is a lane that: 'in the parish of Merstham retains the name Pilgrims' Lane. It runs in the direction of the chalk hills, and was the course taken by pilgrims from the west who resorted (as indeed from all parts) to Canterbury.'[27] The second reference to the Pilgrims' Road in Surrey is at Titsey and Tatsfield, where according to Manning and Bray, the 'Pilgrims' Road (so called from the passage of pilgrims to the shrine of St. Thomas a Becket at Canterbury) which is now perfect, not nine feet wide and still used as a road'.[28]

4

From Pilgrims' Way to North Downs Way

Folklore Along the Way

One can find many historic sites along the trail that are associated with the folklore of pilgrimage. Boughton Aluph church has a porch with a chimney and fireplace on its southern flank. Local folklore suggests that pilgrims gathered in the porch for warmth and refuge until their numbers were large enough to ascend up into King's Wood in safety. The short history of All Saints church has an interesting paragraph about the porch:

> The recently re-opened south porch contains a feature which is believed to be unique and may be attributable the church's historic position astride the Pilgrims' Way. The porch was adapted as a shelter for wayfarers by the building of a beautiful Tudor style fireplace with a herringbone hearth and backing. It is said that on the last stage of the journey from Winchester to Canterbury, pilgrims rested here until there were enough of them to brave the onward road through King's Wood, which was known to be infested with robbers.[1]

However, Sean Jennett has suggested that the porch may have been added as a vestry or private room. Other commentators have noted that the porch may have been added in the sixteenth century and, as such, it may have been seen by few pilgrims because it may well post-date the Reformation.

As the trail emerges from King's Wood, one gets what is believed to be the first view that pilgrims had of Canterbury Cathedral's Bell Harry tower as they descended across the sweep of the Downs into what is now Godmersham Park and looked north-east along the Stour Valley. However, only pilgrims

23 Carved Pilgrims' crosses at
St Martha's Chapel, St Martha's
Hill, near Guildford

24 Carving of pilgrims' scallop
shell, St Martha's Chapel

travelling in the last few decades of pilgrimage would have glimpsed the Bell Harry tower as it was not built until between 1490 and 1498.

A popular notion pertains to the rough marks or crosses carved into the walls of churches, which have become known as pilgrims' crosses. Wilfrid Hooper noted that such crosses are often found in in the entrance doorway of churches and also on the nave pillars.[2] Examples of pilgrims' crosses are found along the Pilgrims' Way in Canterbury Cathedral, the north doorway of Compton church, as well in stonework in St Martha's chapel, near Guildford. The crosses often have an additional arm struck across that are said to have been carved by pilgrims once they had completed their pilgrimage, presumably when they passed by upon their return journey, or by those who originated from that particular parish. Examples of carved pilgrims' crosses with the additional arm struck across them are on display in St Martha's chapel and can be seen in the photograph on page 65.

However, both Wilfrid Hooper and Elliston-Erwood concluded that there was no evidence to link such marks with pilgrims and it has been suggested that these could also be Masons' marks or banker marks. In Sussex such marks were known as crusader marks and are believed to have been carved by those returning from the crusades.

Another common local belief is that the large snails found along the Pilgrims' Way close to Charing were originally introduced to the area by Norman pilgrims who dropped them as they made their way along the trail. Cartwright talks about traces of the pilgrims' presence remaining to the present day and makes reference to the snails found along the way at both Albury in Surrey and at Charing in Kent.[3] The particular variety is the *helix pomatia*, or Apple snail, and is usually known as the Roman snail in England due to its likely introduction into southern England by the Romans. Today it can be found in chalk and lime habitats, which explains its occurrence on the edge of the chalk escarpment. When climatic conditions are right so many of these snails appear on the Pilgrims' Way that it can be hard to take a step without crushing them underfoot. Nevertheless, H.S. Ward, in *The Canterbury Pilgrimages*, notes that stories of the existence of the Roman snails abound throughout the southern counties.[4]

A similar common view repeated by many is that the way can be identified by the ancient yews that mark its course. Belloc, whilst not going as far as claiming that yews were planted to mark the course of the Way, does make much of the yews as a sign to identify the course of the old road: 'Such evidences were the well-known fact that a line of very old yews will often mark such a road where it lies upon the chalk.'[5]

Certainly, there are many sections of the Pilgrims' Way that are lined by yew trees which, like snails, prosper in areas of chalk, and it is often a useful method

25 East flanking wall of Archbishop's Palace, Charing

of identifying a green lane or bridleway. Nevertheless, whilst both Belloc and Cartwright make much of the presence of yews found along the Pilgrims' Way, neither claims any direct link between yew trees and the Pilgrims' Way. Julia Cartwright is quite categorical about this point when she states that:

> So striking is this feature of the road, and so fixed is the idea that some con-nection exists between these yew trees and the Pilgrims' Way, that they are often said to have been planted with the express object of guiding travellers along the road to Canterbury. This, however, we need hardly say, is a fallacy. Yews are by no means peculiar to the Pilgrims' Way, but are to be found on every road in chalk districts.[6]

Jennett makes the point that many writers have connected the Pilgrims' Way with the lines of yews to be found along the chalk escarpment. In fact, he goes on to suggest that few yews found along the wayside are more than a couple of hundred years old and that the age of yew is greatly misunderstood for the reason that 'several stems which fuse into one, and the thickness that results is often misleading'.[7] So local stories and beliefs can present a number of problems and we need to be aware of how useful these are as historical evidence. A locally held view, irrespective of the fact that it is widely held and has been passed on verbally, is only folklore if it can be shown to predate its written introduction. Rackham reminds us that 'aged countrymen, like the rest of us, enjoy a good story and do not always separate what they have read from what they have seen; and are tempted to guess at explanations of what they do not know'.[8]

26 Ruins of the
Archbishops Palace,
Charing

27 Further ruins of the
Archbishops Palace,
Charing

Growth in Criticism of Pilgrimage

Following the dissolution of the monasteries, Henry VIII turned his attention to the wealth of the shrines. There had by this time already been a number of critics of pilgrimage and in particular the cult of Becket. These included in Chaucer's era, John Wycliffe, a dissident theologian who criticised the wealth the shrine brought to the monks. His followers, referred to as Lollards, were an outspoken group extremely critical of the excesses of pilgrimage and, in 1530, one such Lollard, William Umpton, was imprisoned for asking why Becket should be a saint rather than Robin Hood.

In September 1538 Henry VIII ordered the King's Commissioners to sack the saint's shrine and remove the bones of Becket. Furthermore, the donations of pilgrims were removed and transferred to the king. John Ure states that after 1538 'no longer could disparate bands of pilgrims, such as Chaucer's, find a worthy and commendable reason for making a spring jaunt to Kent'.

Certainly by the latter half of the fourteenth century many of us, if we had been alive at the time, might have been critics of pilgrimage. For instance, Langland's *Piers the Ploughman* tells pilgrims that they should seek the blessed Saint Truth rather than going on pilgrimages. Similarly, some commentators have interpreted Chaucer as being critical of pilgrimage because the *Canterbury Tales* illuminates aspects of pilgrimage that attracted anti-pilgrimage sentiment, expressed by puritan groups such as the Lollards. The Kent Heresy Proceedings of 1511–12 demonstrate that right across the county, many of those who came from towns and villages on or close to the Pilgrims' Way were dissenters who held that pilgrimage and the veneration of images were idolatrous practices.

The Pilgrims' Way after the Pilgrimage

What happened to the ancient trackway if pilgrimage ceased in the middle of the sixteenth century? Christopher Taylor suggests that the Highways Act of 1555, which stipulated that parishes were responsible for the upkeep of roads within their area of jurisdiction, was the first important step towards state control of the roads.[9] It is at this time that roads start to be marked on county and national maps. Symonson's map, *A New Description of Kent* (1596), shows main roads through Kent, of which most follow the line of the existing Roman roads. In relation to the Pilgrims' Way, no road is shown as leaving from the west of Kent below (i.e. further south) the line of Watling Street.

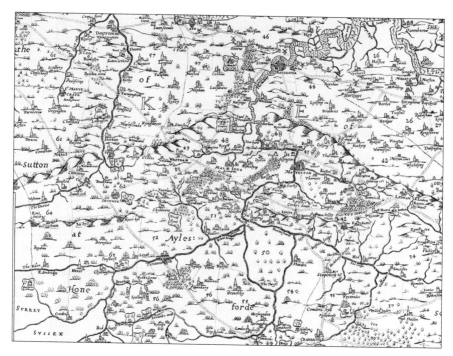

28 Symonson's Map of Kent, 1596 (reproduced with kind permission of the Centre for Kentish Studies)

Attempts at enforcing parishes to maintain adequate roads failed to have much impact. Subsequently, an Act of Parliament in 1663 allowed, for the first time, Justices of the Peace to levy tolls on sections of the Great North Road to contribute towards its upkeep. Throughout the eighteenth century the state's involvement through legislation aimed at encouraging the creation of turnpike trusts started to encourage private investment in the road network. Taylor informs us that by 1821 it has been estimated that over 18,000 miles of English roads had been turnpiked.[10]

It has been argued that, as the toll road system developed, travellers reverted to using the old trackways to avoid paying the tolls. We have already seen that Albert Way's essay of 1855 refers to one such trackway when he cites the Rev. Pearson's knowledge of the Pilgrims' Road being an ancient trackway running parallel to and above the Ashford to Canterbury turnpike road.[11]

William Cobbett, in his letters, recommended that travellers leave the toll roads and explore the old trackways, and wrote, 'those that travel on turnpike roads know nothing of England'. Another reason for using the old tracks along the edge of the Downs is that many of the chalk slopes were not cultivated and, as such, allowed travellers to pass without trespassing on tilled land.

Elliston-Erwood makes the point that one cannot walk far along the old road without noticing numerous chalk pits, many abandoned and others still being worked. He suggests that perhaps the name 'chalk road' would be more appropriate than the 'tin road' that Grant Allen referred to it as. Belloc argues that chalk- and lime-working kept the old road in use. He also adds that later, when the valley roads were developed, chalk pits were extended and would often cut into the route of the old road and exploitation of the pits destroyed the way in places. So Belloc's argument works both ways: as chalk not only saves the road but is also responsible for its destruction in places.

From Pilgrims' Way to National Trail

In many respects, the road has had a brief period of stability in its recent history, since many sections of the Pilgrims' Way became incorporated into a 110-mile stretch of the North Downs Way National Trail between Farnham and Canterbury. It is, however, often the case that the North Downs Way will maintain the high ground along the top of the chalk ridge, whereas the Pilgrims' Way often hugs the lower levels of the escarpment, particularly where the way has become a metalled lane. The new trail also included the 57-mile North Downs loop, of which the northern side follows the Stour Valley between Wye and Canterbury. The loop also offers walkers the alternative of continuing from Wye in an east-bound direction along the edge of the chalk escarpment to Dover. As such, the National Trail enables walkers to continue along stretches of ancient trackway towards Folkestone and the coast, combined with some superb cliff-top walking as the trail approaches Dover. The final link of the loop connects Dover with Canterbury and thereby approximates to the route that medieval travellers may have taken on their journey between Canterbury and mainland Europe. However, Watling Street would have offered the most direct route for pilgrims between Canterbury and the port of Dover.

The National Trail's official opening in 1978 was the culmination of a process that had taken place over a period of three decades, initiated by the lobbying of the Ramblers' Association and a growing recognition that those living in an increasingly urbanised environment needed legitimate forms of access to the countryside. The process of the long-distance route's establishment reflected a gradual change in thinking, which eventually moved away from a rigid concept of the Pilgrims' Way towards a broader North Downs trail.

The wartime Scott Committee on Land Utilisation in Rural Areas heard evidence from the Ramblers' Association which called for the creation of a number of long-distance footpaths. Following on from the work of both the Scott and Dower committees, the Hobhouse Report of the Special Committee on Footpaths and Access to the Countryside (1947) recommended the establishment of a number of long-distance routes.[12]

29 Ruins of St Mary's church, Pilgrims' Way, Eastwell Park

The Hobhouse recommendations for long-distance footpaths were enacted under Section 51 of the National Parks and Access to the Countryside Act (1949). This made general provisions for long-distance routes to enable the public to make extensive journeys on foot or on horseback where the whole or the greater part avoided public roads.[13] A route along the Pilgrims' Way was one of a number of long-distance routes suggested by Hobhouse.

The original consideration of the National Parks Commission had been to commence a route at Winchester.[14] A report in *Country Life* of 2 February 1951 described as laudable Kent County Council's intention to open up and signpost 62 miles of the Pilgrims' Way in time for the Festival of Britain. These signs can still be found in many places along the trail, bearing the name of the Pilgrims' Way alongside an embossed scallop shell. The article made reference to Belloc and the primeval trackway from Salisbury Plain to the Channel ports and the notion of pilgrims from Winchester joining the trackway at Farnham. However, in the following month a comment in an internal memo on a Ministry of Town and County Planning file hinted at a possible reason for lack of progress on the part of one county 'may be that they have been informed by the view held in some quarters that the Way is "phoney", but one does not know'.[15] The Countryside Commission's files inform us that by 1952 the proposed Pilgrims' Way route from Winchester to Canterbury had been mapped by the Ramblers' Association Southern Section.[16] However, there was a view that the Winchester to Farnham section was unsatisfactory. Alternative routes were considered, including one from Farnham to Wansdyke via Inkpen Beacon, as well as one to connect with the South Downs. At the Canterbury end of the proposed route, debate continued about whether the route should continue south-westerly to Folkestone or eastward to Sandwich.

By 1963 an increasing degree of flexibility was apparent from the minutes of the commission's Long-Distance Route Committee, with a direct reference to the concept of the Pilgrims' Way as not being immutable:

> the committee agreed that the concept of a Pilgrims' Way, should not be immutable and also that it might be appropriate to have a North Downs bridleway. The committee felt that for the time being at least the proposed route should be called the North Downs Way, but they would not lose sight of the original idea of the historic Pilgrims' Way to Canterbury.[17]

Perhaps a note contained in the Long-Distance Route Committee's files for 23 February 1965, with the suggestion that the intention would be, regardless of the Pilgrims' Way, to find the most scenic ridge walk, demonstrates that by the mid-sixties the broader view of a North Downs Way rather than the Pilgrims' Way prevailed.

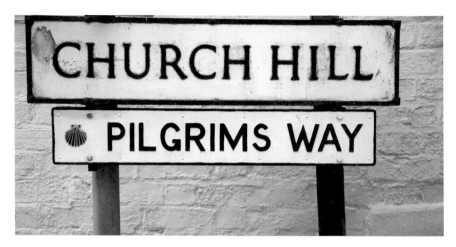

30 Kent County Council sign with scallop shell, Chilham

Nevertheless, the connection with the route and pilgrimage remained strong and in May 1972 the opening of a 43-mile section of the North Downs Way in Kent was celebrated with a Pilgrims' Fayre held in Chilham village. On 30 September 1978, the North Downs Way was officially opened by the Archbishop of Canterbury. Both of these ceremonies suggest that the North Downs Way never found a completely secular route to Canterbury and even from the outset always recognised its co-relationship with pilgrimage.

31 Pilgrims' Way and North Downs Way signs near Lenham

5

The Belloc
and Cartwright Routes

The Italian Art Critic and the French Writer

Perhaps it is less surprising, considering the criticism both later received, that the two writers who did most to re-invigorate interest in the Pilgrims' Way were neither archaeologists nor particular specialists in the field, although both undoubtedly shared a passion for history. Cartwright was already gaining a reputation as an art critic and historian of the Renaissance. Her first book, *Mantegna and Francia*, was published in 1881, two years prior to the publication of the *Pilgrims' Way from Winchester to Canterbury*. Following her marriage, her books carried her married name of Mrs Henry Ady below her maiden name.

Hilaire Belloc spread his talents widely and had been President of the Oxford Union. He gained first-class honours in history from Balliol, served as a Liberal MP for Salford South between 1906 and 1910, and wrote on numerous subjects such as travel, history, politics and religion. He courted controversy throughout his life and has been accused of being both anti-Islamic and anti-Semitic.

Possibly the most damning piece of criticism aimed at their respective books came from Captain H.W. Knocker, who, writing in *Archaeologia Cantiana*, pronounced that 'The present writer has studied with some care the exhaustive treatises of Mr Belloc and Mr Hope Moncrief, not to mention those of Mrs Ady and General James, but their conclusions are based on arguments many of which can only be termed fantastic.'[1]

Irrespective of his criticism, Captain Knocker did suggest that as Kent formed the nearest point of communication with the rest of Europe, one would expect to find a west–east highway running across the county to the coast, although he is clearly of the view that from Canterbury its route took

the line of Watling Street and went via London. Knocker did accept many of
Belloc's arguments for the strategic positioning of Canterbury, serving as it
did the east Kent coastal ports. However, with regard to the Pilgrims' Road,
he suggests that whilst the trackways along the north flank of the Holmesdale
Valley were some of the earliest affecting the valley, they were developed for
the use of local residents and provide east–west linking trackways to reach the
fords and the river valleys of the Darenth and Medway running due north.[2]

Knocker does concede that 'we can piece together stretches of different
roadways, which may well have been used as one'.[3] However, as a final retort to
the pilgrimists, he informs his readers that a further road ran from Maidstone
to the Surrey border, which was 'probably of more importance' and 'attracts
little attention from the authors cited'.[4] But, as we have seen, Symonson's
map of Kent, 1596, does not show a continuous road running westward to
the Surrey border from Maidstone, and certainly does not include a road due
west of the Bromley to Rye road, which Knocker refers to as the route or
droveway running in a south-easterly direction traversing the Wealden Forest.

Cartwright's choice of the Pilgrims' Way was an interesting diversion for
an author whose historical publications were primarily concerned with art
and the history of the Italian Renaissance. Her works included publications
on Raphael, Botticelli, the Italian courtier, diplomat and author, Baldassare
Castiglione, as well as books on Italian gardens of the Renaissance and Isabella
d'Este, Marchioness of Mantua. Art, however, remained a key theme for Julia
Cartwright on her journey along the Pilgrims' Way, as she devotes much of
the book to describing the collections held in the grand houses found close to
the trail. A substantial part of the additional material included in Cartwright's
1911 revised addition of the Pilgrims' Way provides details regarding houses
and their collections, such as the additional four pages devoted to the writer
and diarist, John Evelyn, and his house at Wotton.

Following the Cartwright and Belloc Routes

The flowcharts in the Appendix plot the routes taken by Cartwright and
Belloc between Winchester and Canterbury. These can be used as aids for
anyone planning to walk the Pilgrims' Way and should be used in conjunction
with ten Ordnance Survey Explorer Maps 1:25000 scale: No 132 Winchester;
No 133 Haslemere and Petersfield; No 144 Basingstoke; No 145 Guildford
and Farnham; No 146 Dorking, Box Hill and Reigate; No 147 Sevenoaks and
Tonbridge; No 148 Maidstone and the Medway Towns; No 137 Ashford; No
149 Sittingbourne and Faversham; No 150 Canterbury and the Isle of Thanet.

Julia Cartwright's route is shown in the left-hand column and Hilaire

32 Burham Church, east side of Medway crossing

Belloc's route is shown in the right-hand column. Where the two coincide is shown in the middle column. Sections of their routes that overlap or run very closely to either the Swithun's Way or the North Downs Way are highlighted in greyscale. Even if one follows the marked trails rather than the Belloc and Cartwright routes, the flowcharts serve as a useful tool for approximating the original routes on the maps or to gauge where the Belloc and Cartwright routes are in relation to the way-marked trails along the way.

The original 1904 edition of Belloc's *The Old Road* contains six fold-out 1 inch to 1 mile maps, each approximately 24 inches wide that show the whole of his route in red. Later editions reduced these to a single fold-out map of much reduced scale, which is far too small for practical route planning. Cartwright's 1893 edition of *The Pilgrims' Way* includes two single-page maps. The first map covers the route between Winchester and Gatton Park and the second map covers from Gatton Park to Canterbury. These maps are too small for detailed route planning, but do contain more detail than that shown on the maps contained in later editions.

Comparisons of the authors' routes show that there is not one purist's route to be adopted as the true Pilgrims' Way. Likewise, later writers such as Edwin Hart and Sean Jennett introduced further variations with regard to sections of the route. As such, a strict classification of what is defined as the Pilgrims' Way varies according to what we read. This is a factor that should be considered if one is deciding whether to follow the North Downs Way or sections of the journey signposted as the Pilgrims' Way.

6

Medieval Travellers on the Pilgrims' Way

The Problems Identifying the Routes taken by Medieval Travellers

Perhaps C.G. Crump's concluding shot at discounting the medieval use of the Pilgrims' Way in an article for *History* offers a useful basis upon which to make an appraisal of both the trackway's validity as a principal route between Winchester and Canterbury and any evidence that medieval travellers actually used such a route. This is exactly what Crump asked when he posed the question 'is there any evidence that anyone ever travelled by that route from Winchester to Canterbury?' Of course the route Crump was referring to, in the broadest terms, is the Cartwright and Belloc route from Winchester through the Worthys, Alresford, Alton and Farnham. From here medieval travellers could pick up the North Downs escarpment at Guildford to continue due east across southern England until the Stour Valley, thereafter taking a north-easterly course to Canterbury.

Despite what was described as his trenchant criticism of the pilgrim theory, Crump offered no evidence of itineraries for medieval travellers in support of an alternative route and, as such, he retreats to guesswork when he states:

> How did they go? I do not know, but I can make a guess. In the fourteenth century they went from Winchester to Alresford not by the lanes up the Itchen Valley among the Worthys, but by a straight road over the downs, and so by Alton and Farnham to Guildford. From Guildford they went up to London by Ripley and Kingston, as men go today; and from London they went, like Chaucer's pilgrims, to Canterbury. And that is the road marked on the fourteenth century map in the Bodleian Library, of which Richard Gough published a facsimile in the last volume of his British Topography in 1780.[1]

Not only does Crump fail to offer one alternative itinerary, he admonishes the pilgrimists for their lack of evidence whilst at the same time acknowledging that even where itineraries exist, 'it is not often one can be quite sure which road they went along'.[2] In many respects, Crump's statement highlights one of the real problems with linking medieval pilgrimage with a particular route. Itineraries are few and far between, but just as important is the lack of detail about the exact routes travellers followed between the major towns listed on itineraries or shown by the early cartographers. Paul Hindle, an expert on medieval roads, reminds us that 'documentary evidence is sparse and often of a negative kind, such as the reference to impassable roads in court cases'. For the most part the movement of private individuals is only occasionally recorded and, as Hindle notes, the 'most complete itineraries, however, are those compiled for the kings'.[3] Nevertheless, even the itineraries of kings often lack the detail required to make positive identification of the exact roads they would have followed.

Another problem is that the roads we see on maps today often date back no further than to the development of the turnpike roads in the eighteenth century, which injected capital into the transport infrastructure and produced engineers of the like of Metcalf and Macadam. Christopher Taylor, one of Britain's leading field archaeologists, informs us: 'With the exception of the properly engineered Romans Roads, all roads and tracks in use before the eighteenth century, and in many cases up until the early years of this century, had no proper surface. As a result they were deeply rutted, pot-holed and thoroughly inconvenient to use.'[4]

For instance, today's modern road from Winchester to Guildford is the A31; however, much of the road between Winchester and Alton only dates back some 200 years to the construction of the turnpike road in the eighteenth century.[5] The on-going work of David Weston and David Calow does much to show that there is sufficient evidence to suggest that a Roman road east of Winchester existed, yet for the most part surviving traces have remained elusive.[6]

The Itinerary of Edward I

The record of Edward I's travels throughout his kingdom between 1272 and 1307, compiled in two volumes by Henry Gough and published in 1900, demonstrates only too well some of the problems historians face.[7] As Hindle remarks, itineraries 'provide direct evidence of peoples movements, rather than the simple physical existence of roads'.[8] As such, whilst they tell us much they may fail to pinpoint the detail we need to identify the particular routes taken between one town and the next.

Interestingly, Crump omits to mention Edward's itinerary, despite the fact that many commentators argue it offers documentary evidence to suggest that he may have travelled along the North Downs trackways in Kent. Nevertheless, whilst Edward I is considered by many authorities as being one of the best kings for this kind of evidence, the itineraries undoubtedly raise as many questions as they answer.

Edward's itinerary for August 1289 informs us that the king landed at Dover and undertook a pilgrimage to the shrines of some of England's best-known saints. During the pilgrimage the king's entourage travelled from Dover to Canterbury, Maidstone and Leeds Castle before crossing the Medway to Rochester en route to Essex, Suffolk and Norfolk. From the itinerary we know he sailed to Dover from Whitsand, Picardy, on Friday 12 August, leaving Dover for Canterbury on Sunday 14 August, whereupon he stayed for two nights before leaving for Leeds Castle on Tuesday 16th, then returned to Canterbury the following day, only to travel back to Leeds Castle on Thursday 18 August, where he stayed for 10 nights. Edward then left Kent, avoiding London, and crossed the Thames by boat to Benfleet on Tuesday 30 August, and continued the short distance on to Rayleigh Castle.[9]

Despite the detail of Edward's itinerary, it does not provide evidence that enables identification of the roads taken by his entourage. Commenting on the problems of identifying road routes from royal itineraries, Christopher Taylor, author of *Roads and Tracks of Britain*, points out:

> He [Edward] began by moving directly to Canterbury, presumably along the old Roman road which linked the two places and which is the modern A2. He then travelled west across the North Downs to the manor of Leeds near Maidstone. Here it is possible that the king and his retinue followed the old Pilgrims' Way south east above the River Stour and then, north of Ashford, turned north-west and kept to the edge of the high ground, still along the Pilgrims' Way, to Hollingbourne where he would have descended to Leeds. If this is so we can certainly trace his way along the tracks and green lanes that exist here. On the other hand it is equally possible that the king took the more direct route, followed today by the A252 to Charing and thence along the modern A20 at the foot of North Downs.[10]

Edward's itinerary on this occasion certainly does not show that the royal party used the Pilgrims' Way further west of the Medway Gap, although he may have used the Pilgrims' Way in Kent between Canterbury and the Medway. Neither does it offer conclusive evidence that the royal entourage opted for the Pilgrims' Way rather than lower tracks through the Vale of Holmesdale or

33 Gate to Archbishop's Palace, Charing

the along the greensand ridge towards Leeds Castle. It is evident that by the sixteenth century, from Philip Symonson's map of Kent (1596), a trackway existed from Canterbury to Charing via Chilham and above Challock. This trackway is shown as continuing along the vale west of Charing, passing south of Lenham and crossing the Medway at Aylesford before crossing the Darenth at Chepsted.

Four years before his 1289 visit to Leeds Castle, Edward had approached Kent from the west. According to evidence contained in the records of the Privy Seal and the Patent Roll, on Saturday 13 January 1285 Edward arrived at Guildford and the following day journeyed to Wotton. The day after he continued to Reigate, arriving at Leeds Castle on Friday 19 January 1285, and finally reaching Canterbury the next day. It would appear from the itinerary that on this particular occasion Edward I chose not to go via Crump's favoured route from Guildford to London and thereafter along Watling Street, as Chaucer's pilgrims would nearly a century later, but instead took a route due east of Guildford, stopping at towns just below the North Downs escarpment, across Surrey and into Kent. So Edward's itinerary offers evidence of a medieval traveller who not only crossed the country from Guildford without going through London, but also did this in the middle of winter, arriving at Canterbury on Saturday 20 January 1285.

It should also be noted that the route from Guildford to Canterbury, through London via Ripley and Kingston, is identical in distance when compared with the route along the Pilgrims' Way. Both are approximately 82 miles and this is an important factor when comparing the two routes. Critics of the Pilgrims' Way often refer to alternative routes being direct, less laborious or more convenient, yet none have offered a comparison of the actual distances involved.

The itinerary also tells us that Edward used the Farnham–Ripley–Kingston–Westminster route, commencing on Friday 17 September 1294. This is the road to London that follows a red route on the 1370 Gough map and is the route to which Crump refers. We also know that on occasions Edward would use Watling Street between Westminster and Canterbury. On 15 March 1300 he travelled to Canterbury calling at Erith–Swanscombe–Rochester–Newington–Ospringe, arriving at Canterbury on Sunday 21 March 1300.[11]

What Edward's itinerary suggests is that, when need arose, it was feasible to avoid London by taking a route east along the edge of the North Downs to Canterbury. This doesn't prove that he followed the Pilgrims' Way, but it is evidence of one medieval traveller who opted to travel between Guildford and Canterbury, passing through towns and villages along the edge of the North Downs, when he wasn't required at Westminster. Moreover, on occasions Edward's times in Canterbury coincided with the summer anniversary of Becket's translation.

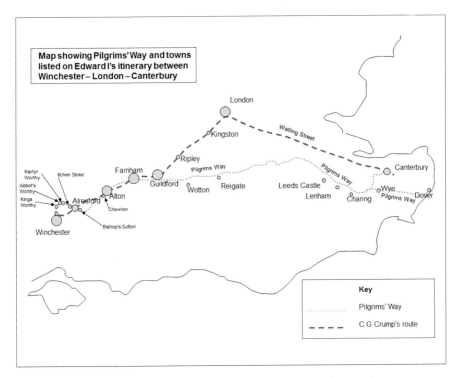

34 Edward I's itinerary where it coincides with the Pilgrims' Way and Crump's route via London

Crump's guess about the choice of route taken by medieval travellers between Winchester and Canterbury is far from robust for two other reasons. Firstly, he asserts that 'from London they went, like Chaucer's pilgrims, to Canterbury. That is the road marked on the fourteenth century map in the Bodleian Library, of which Richard Gough published a facsimile in the first volume of his British Topography in 1780.'[12] But, unfortunately, whilst the Gough map does show the route from Guildford through Ripley and Kingston to London marked by a red line, it omits any route east of London towards Canterbury. In fact, the Gough map, which was probably drawn in a period of 20 years from 1355, even omits Watling Street and only shows one road through the county of Kent. Terence Lawson, who has recently examined the details of Kent as shown on the Gough map, makes the point that 'there are glaring omissions of well known routes, not least the busy section of Watling Street across North Kent'.[13] Moreover, Lawson makes an interesting observation in respect of pilgrimage and the one red route shown across Kent, when he says: 'The only "red line" route shown in Kent is that which apparently ran between Southampton and Canterbury, through Sussex … It is tempting to surmise that this Southampton–Canterbury route was a popular one for pilgrims from the coastal districts of central southern England to Becket's shrine.'[14]

Examination of the Gough map shows that many of the towns situated on or close to the Pilgrims' Way, such as Reigate, Otford and Charing, are given as much prominence as many of the towns linked by the red routes.

Secondly, and to be fair to Crump, he didn't have the benefit of seeing the development of Britain's motorway system from the late 1960s onwards. If he had, then with hindsight he may have revised his conclusion that when travelling between Winchester and Canterbury, 'from Guildford, they went up to London by Ripley and Kingston, as men go to-day'. Today, motorists pick up the motorway at the end of the Hog's Back, just after Guildford, and follow a course just south of the North Downs escarpment. The modern route avoids London altogether.

Finally, before we leave the itinerary of Edward I, it would be remiss not to mention two other journeys from his itinerary. On Friday 11 May 1302 Edward left Winchester for Bishop's Sutton, whereupon he continued to Chawton on Saturday 12 May, Farnham on the next day and Guildford on Monday 14 May.[15] The itinerary also informs us that some years earlier Edward left Farnham on Saturday 18 September 1294 for Westminster and stopped at Ripley and Kingston on the Saturday.[16] This, of course, is exactly as Crump suggests.

There is also evidence that on Monday 7 March 1306, Edward may have travelled by way of the Itchen Valley, on the north side of the river, and towards the Worthys. The Worthys, of which Crump is so dismissive when he says, 'in the fourteenth century they went from Winchester to Alresford not by the lanes of the Itchen valley, along the Worthys, but by the straight road over the downs'. But here we have Edward at Bishop's Sutton, east of Alresford, on Sunday 6 March; at Itchen-Stoke, west of Alresford, on Monday 7 March; and, the following day, back at Winchester and Hyde. Itchen-Stoke places Edward west of Alresford, west of the New Alresford river crossing at Seward's Bridge, shown as Sewer's Bridge on Ogilby's 1675 map (plate 97, scroll 1, London to Poole); and west of the ford at New Alresford. To avoid crossing the Itchen by the ford at Chilland, as well as returning on the right side of the Itchen for Hyde abbey and Winchester's North Gate, Edward could have followed the route through the Worthys back to the city. If this was the case then Edward would have used the route favoured by both Belloc and Cartwright between Itchen-Stoke and Winchester.

In his consideration of the most likely Saxon route or main road between Winchester and Alresford, Cochrane suggests that 'The obvious road, since it involves no crossings of the Itchen, is that from the north gate of the city to Kings Worthy, then bending with the river to the existing track which leaves the B3047 between Martyr Worthy and Itchen Abbas, and till recently led to Abbotstone'.[17]

35 Hyde Abbey Gate,
Winchester

Crump's favoured route to Alresford is, as he states, 'not by the lanes along the Worthys, but by the straight road over the downs, and so by Alton and Farnham too Guildford'. Ogilby's map of 1675 supports this as it shows a road leaving on the left near Winnall Farm, departing the straight road from Winchester's east gate after it has climbed over Magdalen Hill. Ogilby marks this turning off to the left as the Alton road. The route of the road leading east from Winchester, which Ivan Margary believed was a Roman road leaving Winchester's east gate (as mentioned at the beginning of this section), continues to remain elusive beyond Magdalen Hill.[18]

Wilfred Hooper also had an article published in *Surrey Archaeological Collections* in the same year, just prior to the appearance of Crump's article in *History*. He is more specific about the routes between Alresford and Winchester when he states:

Notwithstanding Mr Belloc's 'certitude' that the Way started from the north gate of the city, the probability is that the road to Alresford left by the east gate and passed through Winnall and Easton, keeping to the south side of the Itchen. An alternative route was by the road over Magdalen Hill. Recent excavation at Winnall has revealed the Roman road passing the church in the direction of Easton, and among its merits this route, which still exists, cut the bend of the Itchen and avoided the low lying ground on Mr Belloc's route and the ford at Itchen Stoke. The land leading from Winchester toward Winnall has for centuries past been known as Beggar's Lane, a name which should commend itself to pilgrimists, while pilgrim's badges have been found in this lane by Winnall church.[19]

36 Capital retrieved from Hyde Abbey, Winchester

Yet, notwithstanding the reasons outlined above, Edward's itinerary suggests that on one occasion the king may have travelled by the Saxon track-ways through the Worthys, keeping north of the River Itchen, en route to Winchester and Hyde Abbey. Of course, given the short distances involved in this example, Edward may have simply made separate journeys to and from Winchester each day, and as such any relationship between each location shown on Henry Gough's itinerary becomes largely irrelevant.

Henry II the Penitent Pilgrim

It is the route taken by Henry II upon his return to England following Becket's murder that is probably the royal journey most cited by pilgrimists in support of the direct route between Winchester and Canterbury. For, as Albert Way stated in his essay on the path towards the shrine, 'It has been supposed, with much probability, that Henry II, when he landed at Southampton, July 8, 1174, and made his pilgrimage to Becket's tomb, may have approached Canterbury by this route'.[20]

Dean Stanley described how the wind abated as Henry arrived at the port of Southampton, from where he rode with speed to Canterbury and avoided towns as much as possible, to arrive in Canterbury five days later on 12 July. Stanley suggests that the king's route was via the road, of which traces still remain, that goes over the Surrey Hills and falls into the London Road by the ancient village and hospital of Harbledown. Dean Stanley had discussed the likelihood of this route with Albert Way, for it was Way's essay that he included as an appendix to his *Historical Memorials of Canterbury*.

Others, though, were not so sure about Henry's route to Canterbury. Wilfrid Hooper expressed doubts about Henry's route avoiding London. One reason being was that the Pipe Roll refers to a charge for the hiring of horses for the use of sailors to follow the king to London. Hooper acknowledges this could mean that Henry's servants went direct to London while Henry went via Canterbury, although he adds that this would be by a stretch of language.[21] Although Hooper notes that the chronicler remarks that along the journey Henry confessed his sins and distributed offerings at chapels and hospitals, which leads him to argue that the king's pace allowed little time for such digressions. But Norbert Ohler's book, *The Medieval Traveller*, informs us that the average traveller on horseback, going slowly with followers and baggage, could cover a daily distance of 20–30 miles and the able-bodied rider in a hurry could cover 30–40 miles in one day. This suggests that if Henry used the Pilgrims' Way, which certainly had benefits for a mounted traveller in comparison with the paved Roman roads, then the distance within Henry's four to five day timescale would have been possible.[22]

Henry VIII and the Field of the Cloth of Gold

A little over 200 years after the death of Henry II, another King Henry would pass through Kent along the edge of the chalk escarpment on his way to Canterbury. And it was this king that would effectively bring to an end the age of English pilgrimage and with it the destruction of Becket's shrine. Maybe it was this very journey through Kent en route to France and the Field of the Cloth of Gold, and the memory of the four archiepiscopal palaces passed along the Pilgrims' Way that would be remembered by Henry VIII when he embarked upon the dissolution of the monasteries eighteen years later.

37 North Tower stairwell, Archbishop's Palace, Otford

King Henry's entourage of 3,400 members of the English nobility left
Greenwich on 21 May 1520 and wound its way along the Darenth Valley to
Otford, where it stayed overnight. On the second day they journeyed further east and stayed overnight at Leeds Castle before journeying on to reach
Charing and the archbishop's palace on 23 May. This enormous royal party
descended on Canterbury, where it stayed before making its way to Dover
to depart for France on 31 May. Again, it is difficult to ascertain if Henry's
entourage followed the tracks through the Holmesdale villages or kept well
away from them, maintaining the edge of the hillside and the Pilgrims' Way.[23]
Belloc certainly thought it was the Pilgrims' Way that Henry followed and

informed his readers as such: 'By this road, last of so many, went Henry VIII to the Field of the Cloth of Gold. It was an alternative to Watling Street, and an alternative preferred from its age and dignity.'[24]

The royal itineraries do tell a useful and documented story of travel to Canterbury throughout the period of pilgrimage. They tell us that royal routes sometimes chose to avoid London if they so desired, keeping north of the Kent and Sussex Weald and south of the North Downs. Nevertheless, the exact detail of the routes between the towns and villages mentioned often remain difficult to ascertain. This is the very point that Christopher Taylor highlights with the example of Edward I's movements between Canterbury and Hollingbourne. Did the royal parties use the Pilgrims' Way or did they progress through the vale just as modern travellers do today?

Pilgrimage as Punishment

What other clues exist as to the identities of travellers that may have used the Pilgrims' Way en route to Canterbury in the period of medieval pilgrimage? We know that pilgrimage was used by both ecclesiastical and secular courts as a form of punishment. Imposing pilgrimage upon someone found guilty may have served a number of purposes beyond that of simply redemptive punishment. In effect, imposed pilgrimage meant that the guilty party was effectively removed from the local community for a set period of time and justice was also seen to be done. Often a signed declaration was required from the shrine as proof of having undertaken the stipulated penance upon return to their community.

Canterbury was the most commonly named English shrine in the secular courts in many cities throughout Flanders.[25] Diana Webb refers to a number of pilgrimages imposed as punishment by bishops. Among the examples she cites are three instances where bishops situated at the western end of the Pilgrims' Way imposed penitential pilgrimages to Canterbury. One such pilgrimage was imposed by John Walton, the Bishop of Salisbury, between 1388 and 1395. In May 1308, Henry Woodlock of Winchester imposed a suspended sentence on Robert Urry, who had been part of group of people molesting a vicar. Urry was ordered to undertake a pilgrimage to both Canterbury and Bury without drinking wine on his outward journey.[26] Another Bishop of Winchester, William Wykeham, had to reduce the conditions attached to Elizabeth Juliers, the Countess of Kent's penitential pilgrimage to Canterbury. Diana Webb also lists Simon de Buntingford, described as a farmer and chaplain of the church of the fruits of Ryarsh situated just west of the Medway Gap and close to the Pilgrims' Way, who was ordered to undertake a penitential pilgrimage.

The chaplain was directed to take a pilgrimage, both to the shrine of St Thomas at Canterbury and to St Thomas of Hereford, due to defects in the running of his farm and the fact he was also committing adultery.

Pilgrims Flasks or Ampullae

The ampulla or small lead flask was an important item within the ritual of pilgrimage. Upon reaching the shrine and completion of their journey, pilgrims would purchase small lead flasks, within which they could fill holy water, oil or the blood of the saint. At Canterbury it is believed that the monks maintained a lead cistern that contained Becket's blood, which was continually topped up with a diluted mixture of water and red ochre.[27]

According to the account of William Fitzstephen, one of four narrators who claimed to have been with Becket at the time of his murder, a monk named Arnold was sent to the transept with a basin to collect Becket's blood and brains. Dean Stanley, in his *Historical Memorials of Canterbury* suggests that the collection of the martyr's blood in these small phials became a distinguishing characteristic of the Canterbury pilgrimage:

> A citizen of Canterbury dipped a corner of his shirt in the blood, went home, and gave it, mixed with water, to his wife, who was paralytic, and who was said to be cured. This suggested the notion of mixing the blood with water, which, endlessly diluted, was kept in innumerable vials, to be distributed to the pilgrims;★ and thus, as the palm★★ was a sign of the pilgrimage to Jerusalem, and the scallop shell of the pilgrimage to Compostella, so the leaden vial or bottle suspended from the neck became the mark of a pilgrimage to Canterbury.[28]

It would not be unreasonable to expect ampullae to be unearthed along the course of the Pilgrims' Way. It is certainly the case that they have been found in numerous sites around the country. Documented finds of ampullae recorded by local archaeological societies, as well as the Portable Antiquities Scheme (PAS), a voluntary scheme to record archaeological finds made by members of the public, aid the identification of patterns of finds. Records show that ampullae have been found at sites close to the Pilgrims' Way at Leeds in Kent, Hollingbourne, Lenham, Boxley, Halling, Guildford, Godstone, Bishops Sutton and Winchester.

However, whilst many of these ampullae have identifiable scallop shells designs, some also have the letter W included in their ornamentation, thought to refer to Our Lady of Walsingham. Other commentators suggest that

38 Christ Church Gate, Butter Market, Canterbury

ampullae had a broader usage and such items were not only connected with pilgrimage but served many other functions.

Richard of Southwick the Merchant Pilgrim

An archaeological find that included two ampullae may hold a particular significance for the Pilgrims' Way story. Not only might these ampullae be linked with Canterbury, but more importantly they could be linked with the identity of an individual who we know to have resided in Southampton at the end of the thirteenth century. Archaeologists identified the owner of these ampullae as Richard of Southwick. They have also been able to tell us something of his life. This has been possible because a fire at his house caused the rear of the building to collapse into an adjoining cesspit, effectively sealing the contents of the pit in a time capsule for 700 years.[29]

Richard of Southwick was a merchant and a burgess of Southampton who lived in Cuckoo Lane close to the quayside. It is known from documentary sources that his career spanned the period 1268–90. We also know that he died sometime in 1290 and was survived by his wife and two daughters. In addition to documentary evidence telling us something about Richard's life, archaeological evidence from the pit close to Southwick's house revealed that he was a man with international contacts who traded widely.

Southwick no doubt travelled and traded widely across Europe, because evidence from the pit showed that he had connections with Bernard de Vire, a merchant from Normandy. Colin Platt suggests that this evidence tells us that Richard 'lived extraordinarily well', for he possessed decorated jugs from south-west France and lusterware from Spain. He also enjoyed wines from southern France and had a sheath for a dagger made of Spanish leather. Southwick even had a small monkey as a pet, believed to have originated from North Africa. However, in addition to these items, two ampullae were found that had been bought at Canterbury. As Diana Webb states in *Pilgrimage in Medieval England*, Richard of Southwick or someone in his household 'had gone at least once to Canterbury and brought back two souvenir ampullae'.[30]

Not only is it possible that Richard of Southwick went on at least one pilgrimage to Canterbury, but his journey may have followed in the footsteps of Henry II's penitential pilgrimage to the tomb of Thomas Becket. If this was so then Richard may well have taken the Pilgrims' Way to Canterbury and, as Colin Platt states:

There is evidence also of a visit by Richard of Southwick to Canterbury
later in the same century, where he purchased two ampullae, or badges, as

souvenirs to commemorate his excursion. But the habit of pilgrimage in Southampton as elsewhere was far older than this. In 1174 Henry II had landed at Southampton at the start of his expiratory journey to Canterbury. Pilgrims from Spain and western France followed in the king's tracks, making their way, as he had from Southampton to Winchester and thence by the long land route to Canterbury.[31]

So not only do we have a pilgrim who may have chosen to follow the Pilgrims' Way to Canterbury, but we also know his name, the street he lived in and much about his lifestyle and social background. If Richard had been born a century or so later his trading activities would have brought him into contact with new ideas from northern Europe. He may have developed sympathies with the views espoused by John Wycliffe and the Lollards. He may even have adopted views that were opposed to the practice of pilgrimage and the cult of St Thomas. He may have come to think that the passage to God was a personal journey made throughout one's life rather than through the veneration of relics and papal indulgencies to offset an individual's time in purgatory.

However, Richard of Southwick was a man of the thirteenth century and, as someone who was able to generate wealth through his trading activities, he was also in a position to determine how he used his time. For Richard the choice of undertaking an extended period of travel was something that could be accommodated within his lifestyle. At some time in his life he chose to go on pilgrimage to Canterbury and the shrine of Thomas Becket.

To reach Canterbury, Richard may have sailed along the coast from Southampton to the port of Dover or Sandwich. Alternatively, he may have taken the red route shown on the Gough map between Southampton and Canterbury, of which Terence Lawson suggests it 'is tempting to surmise that this Southampton–Canterbury route was a popular one for pilgrims from the coastal districts of central southern England to Becket's shrine'.[32] Of course, Richard of Southwick may have chosen the Pilgrims' Way and followed the route claimed to have been taken by Henry II when he arrived in Southampton in July 1174. As such, Richard of Southwick may well be the closest we have come to identifying an actual pilgrim who could have used the Pilgrims' Way and of whom there is sufficient evidence to link him with the Canterbury pilgrimage.

Trying to establish the route of Southwick's journey to Canterbury mirrors the problems of defining the story of the Pilgrims' Way, precisely for the reason that so much of it is left to conjecture. Perhaps Richard made his pilgrimage via Winchester, travelling along the valleys of the Itchen and then the Wey to Guildford and from there eastwards along the chalk escarpment until reaching the Stour Valley. From there he may have taken a course due

39 The Ford at New Alresford, Pilgrims' Way

north-east towards his final destination of Canterbury, but we cannot tell the route that he took. Neither can we be sure of the exact roads and trackways he would have followed, had he chosen to follow the Pilgrims' Way.

It is presumed that a Roman road ran between Winchester and Neatham, but for the most part evidence of it still eludes archaeologists today.[33] Whether Southwick would have followed a Roman road or one of the medieval roads established by the thirteenth century we cannot tell. Certainly the accounts of seventeenth-century writers, such as John Aubrey and William Camden, told of a Roman road between Alresford and Alton. If Southwick had left Winchester on the route later described by Belloc in *The Old Road* then he would have crossed the Itchen at Itchen-Stoke, whereas had he followed a route as later described by Julia Cartwright in *The Pilgrims' Way*, Southwick would probably have crossed the Itchen at Seward's Bridge. If he had followed the course of the Pilgrims' Way as described by Belloc, then his route would have taken him along Brislands Lane, whereas if he had followed Cartwright's Pilgrims' Way he would have taken a route through Ropley and Rotherfield Park and approached Chawton from the west.

It is apparent that even when we identify pilgrims who have made the journey from Winchester to Canterbury, the historical evidence available does not tell us as yet whether they took the Pilgrims' Way or chose an alternative route. Moreover, if they chose the Pilgrims' Way, then which routes along the way did they take; which of the numerous river crossings did they choose; and did they choose a ridge path or a terrace-way on any particular stretch of their journey? The answers to all these questions remain unanswered.

7

The Paddlesworth Choice

The Medway Gap

Within two or three days of their final destination, medieval travellers would reach the biggest breach in the chalk escarpment of their entire journey. Here they would be faced with a number of options in relation to how they crossed the River Medway. The river valley, known as the Medway Gap, is significant because it serves as a focus for revisiting a number of arguments relating to the routes from London and the west of the country. The options such routes presented for medieval travellers and their possible responses are important with regard to how we view each route and their use by pilgrims.

In reassessing the use of the North Downs trackways vis-à-vis the Medway crossings, reference is made to the research undertaken by Patrick Thornhill regarding the Medway's geological features and the changing characteristics of the Medway river crossings.[1] Travellers had to take many additional factors into consideration. These included the difficulties of travel using the North Downs trackways east of the Medway, with consideration of issues such as: the risk of highway crime; the difficulties associated with the right to travel; and suspicion of those that travelled in feudal society. Finally, travellers would of course take into account the actual distances of the various options before them. The combination of these factors was undoubtedly key in determining why medieval travellers may have favoured one route over another. It is this decision that the author has termed 'the Paddlesworth choice'.

Without recourse to maps, way-markers or modern navigation aids, early travellers could follow the trackways along the chalk escarpment on the southern edge of the North Downs. We have already considered how such paths may have originally been the preserve of wild animals and later followed by ancient man as he hunted in their tracks.[2] Anyone who has walked the National Trail will know from experience that at the start of each morning one can survey the day's journey that lies ahead, simply by observing the span of the North Down's ridge stretched out before one. These routes evolved, not only because their geological qualities offered good drainage, firm ground underfoot and relative ease of passage, but also for the very reason that their natural and recognisable characteristics served as obvious navigation aids.

To the south of the chalk escarpment another geographical feature influenced the route taken by early travellers. Here was to be found the vast expanse of the Weald or forest of Kent and Sussex. For the prehistoric traveller the Weald presented itself as an unknown wilderness. This huge tract of wilderness and woodland followed the southern flank of the North Downs for 90 miles between Lympne, in the east of Kent, through to Petersfield, in east Hampshire. The *Anglo-Saxon Chronicle* recorded that this wood was known as Andredesleag and it continued to be known as Andredsweald up until 1018.[3] The stated size of the Saxon Weald was 120 miles long and 30 miles broad, which according to Peter Brandon would have 'extended it westwards across Hampshire into the New Forest'.[4]

Until recently the prevailing view was that the Andredsweald was a fairly impenetrable forest. Mark Anthony Lower informed his readers in 1870 that Bede described 'the whole of Anderida as all but inaccessible, and the resort of large herds of deer, and of wolves and wild boar'.[5] But current research suggests that the Wealden area was more similar to 'wood pasture than a solid block of impenetrable woodland'.[6] Nevertheless, the Weald still presented numerous difficulties for the early traveller, which undoubtedly made the geographical and geological features of the chalk scarp the obvious choice of passage for those travelling across southern England from or to the west.

There are four breaches in the North Downs' escarpment, each the product of river erosion that formed the valleys of the Wey, Mole, Medway and Stour as they cut paths through the soft chalk downland. But it is the breach in the downs carved by the River Medway, known as the Medway Gap, which presents the largest natural obstacle for any traveller following the trackways running along the chalk scarp between the Surrey Hills and Folkestone.

The Approach to the Medway Valley

The Trottiscliffe to Snodland stretch of the Pilgrims' Way offers both extensive sections of ridgeway and terrace-way. This stretch passes very close to the ancient Neolithic megaliths known as the Coldrum Stones, as discussed earlier, which lie about 200 metres to the south of the trackway, just after the vil-

1 Cliffs – exposed cross-section of chalk downland, near Folkestone

2 Itchen valley,
north-east of
Winchester

3 Millstream at Hyde
Abbey, Winchester

4 Saxon church, Headbourne Worthy

5 Saxon church, Headbourne Worthy

6 Footbridge over the Itchen, Martyrsworthy, illustrated in Julia Cartwright's *The Pilgrims' Way*

7 Civil war musket bullets, St Lawrence church, Alton, near Pilgrims' Way

8 St Martha's chapel, St Martha's Hill, near Guildford

9 St Martha's chapel, near Guildford

10 Coldrum Stones near Trottiscliffe looking east into Medway Gap

11 Medway Gap, Birling ridge

12 Snodland Church from Burham

13 Kits Coty House
looking west into Medway
Gap

14 Pilgrims' Way and
North Downs Way signs

15 Pilgrims' Way west of Lenham

16 Pilgrims' Way above Lenham

17 Pilgrims' Way east of Lenham

18 Pilgrims' Way west of Charing

19 Godmersham Park from King's Wood

20 Black Prince's
Well, Harbledown

21 Canterbury Cathedral from St Edmonds school

22 Canterbury Cathedral

23 Bell Harry Tower, Canterbury Cathedral

24 Ancient trackway (terrace-way) east of Postling

25 White cliffs – showing straits of Dover

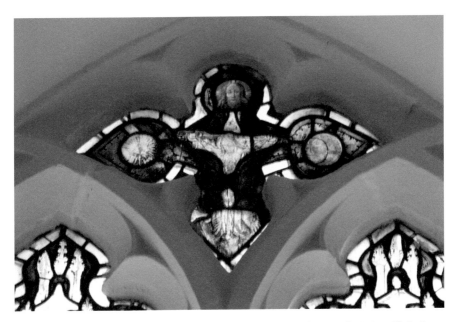

40 St Peter and St Paul's church, Trottiscliffe. Stained glass of dual image depicting Christ in majesty and crucifixion, with the sun and moon, 1342

lage of Trottiscliffe (pronounced Trosley). From here the Pilgrims' Way starts its approach towards the Medway Valley, and begins a gradual curve in a north-easterly arc, following the west bank of the Medway Gap towards Rochester.

The approach into the River Medway is described by Belloc in *The Old Road* and retracing his steps is an excellent way to explore the Medway Gap on foot and to check out Belloc's favoured river crossing at Snodland.[7] The first mile due east from the Trosley Country Park car park follows an upper terrace-way path, which is marked in Old English typeface as the course of a trackway on current Ordnance Survey Explorer maps. After following the higher terrace-way for a mile, take a turning right and descend to a lower terrace-way via a sunken path or hollow-way, eventually emerging at the field line just above the Coldrum Stones. Continue due east along the lower terrace-way at the foot of the escarpment for a further 2 miles before leaving this lower trackway and turning right across a field following a farm track, towards Paddlesworth Farm.

The track leading from the Pilgrims' Way to Paddlesworth Farm is shown on an 1845 tithe map of Paddlesworth as running between Hackett's & Upper Danvil Field and North Field. A survey commissioned by Thomas Wotton of his land in 1559 refers to this connecting trackway as the 'Kings Highway'.[8] A point to note is that Rev. C.H. Fielding, in his *Memories of Malling and its Valley*, includes a map that appears to have been drawn by A.F. Bowker, CE, FRGS.[9] The map is noteworthy because it shows the Paddlesworth Road as directly following the course of the Kings Highway to join the Pilgrims' Way, rather

than continuing west of Paddlesworth Farm to the junction with the Stangate
Road and Birling Hill, as it does today. Both the Andrews, Dury and Herbert
map of 1769 and the Mudge 1-inch Ordnance Survey map of 1801 show a
road connecting Paddlesworth with the Pilgrims' Way. Nevertheless, both the
Andrews and the Mudge maps also show the Paddlesworth Road connecting with the Stangate Road. This does, however, show that the Paddlesworth
Road once served as a thoroughfare linking the Pilgrims' Way with the river
crossing at Snodland.

Julia Cartwright captures the view from the Pilgrims' Way as it approaches
the Medway Gap, when she describes how it:

> continues its course over Wrotham Hill and along the side of the chalk
> downs. This part of the track is a good bridle road, with low grass banks or
> else hedges on either side, and commands fine views over the rich Kentish
> plains, the broad valley of the Medway, and the hills on the opposite shore.[10]

Walking the route today, shelter from the elements is provided by a canopy of
foliage that lines the trackway. Ivan Margary, the leading historian of ancient
British roads, makes the point that 'the southward facing escarpment causes
the terrace-way at its foot to be very hot in summer, when movement along
the Ridgway would have been preferred'.[11] Margary also refers to problems
associated with the ridge of the downs being capped with deposits of clay-
with-flints. He suggests that the terrace-way would be preferable, especially
in winter, so as to avoid a summit that became 'very wet and sticky in rainy
weather'.[12] Margary noted what he later termed as duplication of the North
Downs trackways, where the upper ridge walk would often run in parallel
with a lower terrace-way at the foot of the slope. He argues that prehistoric
travellers would have developed a dual trackway using the upper way in the
summer and the lower way, which is the course that has usually become
denoted as the Pilgrims' Way, in the winter. Given these considerations, the
sheltered terrace-way in winter has an appeal and logic with which it is hard
fault. Nevertheless, for today's walker, in the height of summer the terrace-
way is cloaked with a welcome cover of foliage providing plenty of shade.
Professor Hawkes made an interesting argument that would support this
observation in as much as he regarded 'the lower course as a summer-way'.[13]

However, this section of the trackway may not always have been so shaded.
Jusserand informs us in his work, *English Wayfaring Life in the Middle Ages*, that
in 1285 Edward I introduced legislation that decreed the edges of highways
should be clear and there should neither remain 'coppice nor brushwood nor
hollow nor ditch which might serve as a shelter for malefactors'.[14] Today, in
the summer months, the benefit of the shaded terrace-way is evident and

41 Christ Church Gate, Butter Market, Canterbury

noticeably missed where there are breaks in the shade or if one has to leave the trackway to strike out across open fields, as at Paddlesworth, with reflective chalky soils underfoot. If the Pilgrims' Way was used as a medieval thorough-fare to any great extent, then this present protection from the elements may not have always been evident.

A change of dates upon which Thomas Becket's death was celebrated occurred in the early thirteenth century. Originally the key date was naturally the anniversary of his martyrdom on 29 December 1170. However, following the translation of Becket's relics on 7 July 1220, it would appear from the work of Dean Stanley that this summer date became more popular.[15] Obviously this would make the passage by pilgrims to Canterbury much easier than travelling in the winter months and any shade along this section would have been welcome. However, encouraging mass pilgrimage in July, even once account is taken of the change from the Julian to the Gregorian calendar, seems somewhat at odds with the labour requirements of a primarily medieval rural economy, with second ploughing, sheep shearing and hay making taking place in June and July. This begs the question as to which members of medieval society were actually able to leave the manor to embark on any form of extended pilgrimage.

The Roman Road Alternative

Those of the opinion that medieval pilgrims seldom used the North Downs trackways re-assert their arguments with vigour with regard to the pilgrimage route east of Rochester. Critics of Pilgrims' Way theories tend toward the view that between the Medway and Canterbury, the Roman road, known by the Middle Ages as Watling Street, would have been a traveller's route of choice.

Certainly Roman roads remained a key part of England's road network throughout the Middle Ages. Hindle, in *Medieval Roads*, informs us that there were 8000–10,000 miles of Roman road built by AD 150 that provided a basic network and that very few new roads were built in the medieval period. The Gough map of 1360 includes about 3000 miles of main roads.[16] Medieval roads also had a different character to Roman roads. Hindle states that 'the road was not a physical entity', but was instead a right of way, which would diverge and deviate on to new routes as and when conditions underfoot required.[17]

Therefore a recurring theme in the story of the Pilgrims' Way is the question as to why medieval pilgrims would choose the North Downs trackways in preference to the Roman roads that made up so much of the medieval road network. As Jusserand reminds us: 'There was in England a very considerable network of roads, the principal of which dated as far back as the Roman times.'[18]

The argument in favour of pilgrims using the Roman road network is developed in an essay by E.G. Crump in his criticism of both Brayley's (1850) and Albert Way's (1855) enthusiasm for the Pilgrims' Way. Much of Crump's criticism of pilgrimist theory is discussed earlier, but here we deal specifically with his assertion that medieval travellers would favour Watling Street rather than the Pilgrims' Way. Edward Brayley claimed to have discovered a portion of the trackway crossing the parish of Albury and wrote that 'the ancient path called the pilgrims way, which led from the city of Winchester to Canterbury, crosses this parish, and is said to have been *much used in former times*' (author's emphasis).[19] Crump's scepticism of Brayley's assertion turns to open disagreement when he considers Albert Way's hypothesis, which Crump argues extended what he saw as the misconstrued theory of the North Downs pilgrimage route east of the Medway. Of Albert Way, Crump writes: 'And yet to him, and to no other, is due the great discovery that the Pilgrims' Way did not go to Strood, but crossed the river Medway and took its course along the slope of the downs to Charing and thence to Canterbury.'[20]

Crump's view of the theories expressed by both Brayley and Albert Way is very apparent from his following comments: 'If he had gone further [referring to Brayley's statement in 1850], and surmised that it had once been used by pilgrims from Winchester to Rochester, whence the pilgrims could easily reach Canterbury, it would have been fantastic, but perhaps not absurd.'[21]

Whilst Crump falls short of ridiculing Brayley's contention about the pilgrimage route, it is fairly obvious that he viewed Albert Way's extension of the Pilgrims' Way due east of the Medway and along the North Downs scarp with incredulity. Robert H. Goodsall, who lived close to the trackway at Stede Hill overlooking Harrietsham, east of the Medway, summarised the theme of the detractors when he wrote: 'that there is a good deal of evidence of a negative kind to disprove its use by pilgrims, at all events from the Medway crossing to Canterbury.'[22]

Goodsall, in his *The Ancient Road to Canterbury*, concedes that part of the trackway lying across the western portion of the county may have been used as a pilgrimage route, but repeats the doubts expressed as to whether pilgrims would have continued along the southern flank of the downs. Whilst suggesting that the trackway east of the Medway may well have been used as a long-distance route for the purpose of transporting chalk from the many chalk pits found along the southern flank of the downs, he nevertheless doubts its use as a thoroughfare for pilgrims. Goodsall argues that:

> from the Surrey Kent boundary to Snodland on the Medway, may have been used by Pilgrims coming from the west of England and the shires, but on reaching the latter point, it is far more likely that they would have continued via the trackway which led to Strood and Rochester, crossed over Rochester bridge and journeyed along Watling Street to Canterbury, so joining the main stream of pilgrims coming from the north.[23]

According to Goodsall, one of the reasons why pilgrims would spurn the southern flank of the downs in favour of Watling Street is because the villages along the way lie 'well south of the downland foot, often at a distance of a quarter to half a mile, and weary pilgrims, seeking a night's shelter, would hardly have welcomed the extra toil in reaching them'.[24]

Roadside Crime

There were probably very good reasons why many medieval travellers preferred a route that did not pass directly through areas of population, such as the problems associated with freedom of movement in a feudal society, as well as a greater threat of crime on the main thoroughfares. As Diana Webb notes in *Pilgrimage in Medieval England*, 'whenever they could, pilgrims used well worn tracks which were passable and as secure as possible'.[25] Jack Ravensdale, in his study of the route taken by Chaucer's pilgrims along Watling Street, makes the point that 'in places, however, there were also ancient, often prehistoric trackways which pilgrims might take when they seemed safer or easier than Watling Street'.[26] It is noteworthy that Shakespeare built a sub-plot in *Henry IV* around Falstaff's plans to rob pilgrims on the Gads Hill approach to Rochester. Chaucer alludes to the threat of robbery on Watling Street at Boughton Hill. Other commentators have pointed to the fact that immense pressure could be asserted by sheriffs upon villeins in their role as tithing men at the local level to ensure that culprits were found in cases of wrongdoing. This would often result in the apprehension of strangers whenever a local crime was committed. Ian Mortimer draws on Summerson's *Structure of Law Enforcement*, when he states that: 'If you begin to look at those indicted for serious crime, it soon becomes apparent that many of them are strangers. In some places as many as thirty per cent of all suspected murderers and thieves are described as vagrants.'[27]

Restrictions on Free Movement

Throughout the Middle Ages there were numerous attempts by monarchs to enact legislation to prohibit the lower ranks in feudal society from leaving the land and taking to the roads. Jusserand informs us that the Commons of the Good Parliament in 1376 renewed prohibitions against going out of a man's 'own district'.[28] In 1388–89 statute was enacted in response to labour shortages and vagabondage, which forbade movement by people who served and laboured without testimonial letters justifying their movements. Diana Webb quotes from a Statute of the Realm under Richard II, which stated:

> no servant or labourer, be he man or woman, shall depart at the end of his
> Term out of the Hundred, Rape or Wapentake where he is dwelling, to

serve or dwell elsewhere, or by Colour to go from there in Pilgrimage, unless he bring a Letter Patent containing the cause of going and the Time of his return, if he ought to return, under the King's Sea.[29]

It would appear that those from the lower ranks in society faced the risk of being mistaken for peasants out of bond when travelling. Jusserand noted that during the fourteenth century, laws existed to prohibit the villein leaving his master's domain without special licence and argues that 'escaped peasants brought the most numerous recruits to the wandering class'.[30] The ancient trackway along the North Downs, which passes just above all the spring-line villages but not through them, may therefore have offered a safer as well as more discreet alternative for many medieval travellers en route to Canterbury.

Finally, recent arguments have been put forward to suggest that Duke William's conquest of Kent in 1066 and his army's subsequent passage to London followed the terrace-way along the side of the North Downs, rather than marching up Watling Street and crossing the Medway at Rochester. The hypothesis for this is based upon an 'unexplained decrease in the fiscal value of certain manors as set out in the Domesday Book'.[31] Such a decrease in fiscal value is presumably the resulting effect of an army in transit and the consequential damage to land, crops and buildings left in its wake. So despite the view that the route east of the Medway presented difficulties for small groups of pilgrims, it would appear to some that it presented less of a problem for an invading army. Similarly, Nigel Nicholson suggests that in AD 43 the Roman army advanced on a broad front that incorporated the North Downs from the line of Watling Street to the north and the Pilgrims' Way along the southern edge of the Downs.

Was the Pilgrims' Way the Longer Route?

Notwithstanding the above arguments, it is clear that there is a body of opinion that holds the view that pilgrims would not have opted for what has been described as the 'more laborious route' along the Pilgrims' Way as an alternative to using the old Roman road between Rochester and Canterbury. As such the critics of the North Downs route point to the fact that Watling Street takes a straight continuous course between Rochester and Canterbury as opposed to deviating south along the Medway Valley, then east along the foot of the North Downs escarpment, then back up in a north-easterly direction along the west bank of the Stour Valley, only to rejoin Watling Street within a mile or so of Canterbury.

Even Julia Cartwright, one of the first in the pilgrimist tradition, was prepared to lose a few pilgrims to the Watling Street route when she said some
'might, if they pleased, go on to Rochester, three miles higher up, and join
the London pilgrims along the Watling Street to Canterbury – the route of
Chaucer's pilgrimage'.[32]

It would appear that Cartwright was, in fact, merely restating the thoughts
of Captain E.R. James, when he wrote in 1871:

> But it will be well to state that on arriving at Cuxton, in Kent, the difficulty
> of crossing the River Medway would induce many to continue their jour-
> ney about three miles down the river to Rochester, where they would fall
> into the stream of Pilgrims going to Canterbury by the old Roman Road
> Watling Street, known as Chaucer's route from the tabard at Southwark; and
> this would be the easiest way to those who were wise enough to choose it.[33]

The choice of Watling Street or the Pilgrims' Way also concerned Elliston-
Erwood in the revised second edition (1923) and largely rewritten version of
his original *The Pilgrims' Road*. In his chapter that addresses pilgrimage and
its prevalence, Elliston-Erwood notes that: 'Chaucer's pilgrims – who form
the basis of the popular pilgrim notion – are taken as typical, yet they did
not follow the alleged pilgrim route: they came from London along the old
Watling Street.'[34]

Elliston-Erwood, the one-time pilgrimist before committing a self-
confessed volte-face with regard to the claims of the Pilgrims' Way being a
key route of medieval pilgrimage, felt compelled to confess to his readers
that his early enthusiasm for all things medieval had led him 'into accepting
things that never should have been accepted without much more enquiry
than I gave to them'.[35]

Again, in William Coles Finch's *In Kentish Pilgrim Land*, it is suggested that
the way was 'traversed by large numbers of devout pilgrims because of its historic and religious associations'. But Coles Finch also argues that:

> by far the greater number from other parts, including London, traversed
> the Roman road, familiarly known as Watling Street, of Chaucer's pilgrims'
> fame, and kept to it throughout the whole journey to Canterbury, for it was
> more direct, and offered more comfortable conditions of travel and com-
> panionship than did the Pilgrims Way.[36]

Whilst Coles Finch, unlike Goodsall or even Cartwright, does not actually
suggest that pilgrims from the west of England would have necessarily transferred from the Pilgrims' Way on to Watling Street, he does imply that the

Roman road held distinct advantages in terms of directness and was associated with more comfortable conditions of travel. And finally, even Albert Way, in his essay 'The Pilgrims' Way or Path towards the Shrine', made reference to pilgrims leaving the original ancient track to join Watling Street, east of the Medway, when he stated that they 'proceeded along the high ground on the west of the river Medway, towards Strood and Watling Street. This might have been reasonable to suppose, the more convenient mode of pursuing the remainder of the journey to Canterbury.'[37]

Yet, Albert Way goes on to outline a theory that it was 'more probable that the Pilgrims' Way crossed the pasture of the Medway, either at Snodland or Lower Halling', whilst also suggesting that Watling Street for many might present the more convenient route to Canterbury.

These views need to be considered more closely in the context of alternative Medway crossing points upstream from Rochester, as well how other key pilgrimage sites, such as Boxley abbey situated close to the North Downs trackway, influenced the route east of the Medway Gap. Furthermore, travellers' concerns regarding safety and security on Watling Street and the London to Canterbury routes may well have led many to opt for the North Downs route along the ancient trackway for the reasons outlined above. Difficulties associated with the ease of travel, freedom of movement and the practice of hue and cry in medieval society may also have led travellers to opt for the more secluded trackway along the downs, bypassing the spring-line villages unless it was absolutely necessary to visit them.

Finally, closer examination of the actual distances involved shows that the North Downs trackway was not necessarily a less laborious route compared with Watling Street, as Crump and Goodsall suggest. Those approaching the Medway Gap from the west of the country would have to make their choice of crossing at or around Paddlesworth. The distance from this point, which the author has set where the Pilgrims' Way crosses Birling Hill, to the upper crossing at Snodland is 2.2 miles. The distance from Paddlesworth to Rochester Bridge is 6.2 miles. The journey from Snodland to Canterbury using the North Downs trackway is 33.5 miles, whereas the journey from the Rochester Bridge along Watling Street to Canterbury is 27 miles. Therefore a traveller deciding at Paddlesworth whether to take the Watling Street or the North Downs trackway to Canterbury would have the choice of a 33.2-mile journey via Rochester and Watling Street or a 35.7-mile journey via the Snodland causeway and the North Downs trackway. The latter route using the Pilgrims' Way is in fact only 2.5 miles longer than Watling Street. Distance may not therefore have been the primary consideration when making the Paddlesworth choice. This equates to merely one additional hours walking or approximately an additional thirty minutes each day.

An estimation of the distance that pilgrims on foot could cover has been made by Diana Webb, in *Pilgrimage in Medieval England* (2000), in which she states:

> Although probably less well-shod and well-nourished than the modern day recreational walker, the medieval pilgrim may have been hardier and more accustomed to walking in his daily routine, so it does not seem unreasonable to assume that some at least could average between two and three miles an hour over such a path, as a modern day walker will, depending on the state of the going, the energy and fitness level of the individual and the amount of time taken for rest and refreshment.[38]

Webb's assessment is based upon walking through the King's Wood section of the Pilgrims' Way, which is approximately 7 miles from Canterbury. The inclusion of King's Wood in the Pilgrims' Way story owes much to the Rev. W. Pearson, who, in the mid-nineteenth century, informed Albert Way that an ancient track known as the Pilgrims' Road ran above and parallel with the Ashford and Canterbury turnpike road.[39]

This stretch of the Way is usually rutted and muddy throughout the best part of the year. Observations from organising walking holidays along this section of the Pilgrims' Way over a period of 10 years concur with Diana Webb's view of the distance that could be covered by a traveller on foot. Therefore, if a medieval traveller walked at a pace of 3 miles an hour for approximately five to six hours a day, they would complete the journey between Paddlesworth and Canterbury in just two to three days, with only a couple of overnight stops. Moreover, they would bypass most of the spring-line villages at the bottom of the scarp by keeping to the North Downs trackway, as well as keeping Boxley abbey in their itinerary.

In giving further consideration to the route taken by pilgrims east of the River Medway, it is useful to divide travellers into two distinct groups for the purpose of assessing why some would choose the trackway along the edge of the Downs in preference to Watling Street. In the first group (Group A) are included those travellers who commenced their journey to Canterbury from London, as well as all locations north of London. In the second group (Group B) are included those who commenced their journey from locations west of Kent and south of London (see diagram on page 108).

Group B would need to decide which crossing of the River Medway to take shortly after Trottiscliffe, close to the Coldrum Stones, particularly if the Medway was to be crossed within the vicinity of Aylesford or at the southern or upper-most crossing point. An assumption that Group B would have followed the edge of the downs through Surrey and into Kent, rather than take the route from Guildford up to London using the Roman road, has also been made. On this latter point, it should be noted that the Guildford to London Roman road route would appear to be C.G. Crump's preference, which was discussed earlier.

The Five Medway Crossing Points

The decision over which river crossing medieval travellers would have adopted needs to take account of two factors. First, the arguments made by Belloc in the *The Old Road* vis-à-vis the crossing points at Aylesford, Snodland, Upper Halling and Cuxton, albeit that Belloc's arguments are primarily concerned with the evolution of a prehistoric ancient trackway, need to be taken into account. Second, the arguments of Elliston-Erwood, Crump and Goodsall, the proponents of a direct hike along Watling Street once the Medway had been crossed, also need to be considered. In addition, attention should be given to Rochester and the Watling Street crossing for the reason that a bridge of some description existed at Rochester since the time of the Roman occupation. It is believed that Rochester's first medieval bridge dates from about 960 and that earlier wooden medieval bridges were replaced by a stone bridge in 1391.

Therefore the question of where to cross the River Medway has a number of facets, i.e. at least two time frames (medieval and prehistoric), and deals with travellers approaching the valley from two different directions, which we have called Group A (Watling Street) and Group B (Pilgrims' Way). Our question also raises considerations about the characteristics of the river and its surrounding terrain in prehistoric periods and how these factors impacted upon the development of the ancient trackway. This latter point is significant because of the need to address not only the development of a prehistoric trackway but how, once established, it in turn influenced routes adopted in the Middle Ages.

Whilst due cognisance should be taken of Belloc's discussion of four likely Medway crossing points, i.e. Aylesford, Snodland, Halling and Cuxton, Belloc's assessment was in the context of the prehistoric traveller, not the medieval pilgrim.

Belloc acknowledges that post-prehistoric travellers, such as the Romans, had overcome problems associated with the Gault clay in the Medway Gap through building a causeway at Aylesford, but discounts the Aylesford crossing for three reasons – which he describes as being insuperable. To paraphrase Belloc's words, these reasons are:

i the immense width of the valley and qualifies this by adding that the
   valley would be an 'immense tract of uncertain wooded way'
ii the belt of Gault clay that would have to be crossed to reach the ford at
   Aylesford
iii and finally, prehistoric sites such as Kits Coty lie north of the Aylesford
   crossing and therefore 'a man crossing at Aylesford would have to turn
   back upon his general direction'[40]

A number of counter arguments can be made in respect of Belloc's reser-
vations regarding a crossing point near Aylesford. Oliver Rackham suggests
that even by the time of the Roman occupation the English countryside
'can hardly have been much more wooded than it is today'.[41] Moreover, the
upper Medway Valley around Aylesford includes Gault clay mixed with chalk,
which would have encouraged Neolithic land cultivation. As Champion
noted, the Coldrum Stones 'lie on top of well-developed lynchets, which
must have been formed by hill wash from ploughing that took place before
their construction'.[42] Therefore the cultivation of the land probably pre-dated
the construction of the Coldrum Stones. The Coldrum Stones are also situated within the border of the Gault clay belt so there is every likelihood that
the area of Neolithic cultivation stretched considerably further east towards a
Medway crossing point. Given these considerations, there is sufficient reason
to doubt whether 'an immense tract of uncertain wooded way', as Belloc suggests, presented such a problem for the prehistoric traveller.

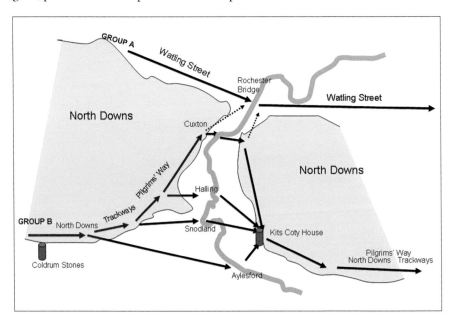

42 The five Medway crossing points

However, if Belloc's concern about the Gault clay still stands, it is equally applied (as Belloc rightly does) to the Snodland crossing. Nevertheless, during the summer months the surface would be passable for the same reason, as Belloc himself argues, for the Gault clay would be hard and dry on the approach to a crossing at Snodland, because it is south facing, and not in the shade of the Holborough knob, as is the case with the approach to a crossing at Halling.

Patrick Thornhill reviewed the Medway crossings of the Pilgrims' Way in an article of the same title, in light of studies undertaken of alluvial deposits in the Medway estuary by J.H. Evans (1953) and R. Kirby (1969), as well as borings taken in the Snodland and Burham area in 1973. Taking account of Evans' and Kirby's earlier work, Thornhill states that 'there has been a striking change in the valley floor since prehistoric times'. Essentially, he argues that the studies of Evans and Kirby show that through the Mesolithic period (10,000–5000 years ago) the sea level rose as the northern ice-sheets melted. The river was shrinking, slowing down and dropping its gravel in its own channel, for it could now carry only its finer sediments down to the advancing sea. This gravel-filled channel, five or six times as wide as the modern Medway at Snodland, was eventually to become the 'buried channel'.

Thornhill also noted that examination of borings taken for the riverside extension of the Snodland paper mills, as well as across the river for a new station of the Medway water board, showed no signs of a Neolithic peat layer at the base of the alluvium deposits and therefore 'it is reasonable to conclude that the surface of the buried channel at Snodland was not covered with alluvium until well after Neolithic times'. This led Thornhill to assert that 'if the Way be older than the megaliths that cluster around it, which can hardly be denied, it must have been well established before the alluvium was deposited and the marshes created'.[43]

Importantly, he goes on to add that the Neolithic Medway 'was not yet tidal and it flowed among the gravel and the sand banks of the channel, which probably split into a number of interlacing streams that could be forded without difficulty'.

Thornhill suggests that for the Neolithic traveller the river was less of an obstacle than the muddy marshland it was to become, whereas, when Belloc was considering the Medway crossing, the prevailing view was that the upper Medway Valley consisted of Gault clay and marshland.

Finally, Belloc's last point regarding turning back upon oneself to reach Kit's Coty House and Boxley is tenuous. The journey from the Coldrum Stones, on the west side of the Medway Gap, to Kit's Coty House, via Aylesford on the east side of the Medway Gap, circumscribes a southerly arc of 6.5 miles in length. Compare this with the Snodland crossing from the same points and

43 Aylesford's fourteenth-century bridge

the distance is 6.2 miles. Even if the topography of the area may have influenced any decision, in spite of the points made above, distance alone can only be considered a marginal factor.

Nevertheless, Thornhill makes reference to the fact that the surface of the gravel of the buried channel is sufficiently thick and extensive to be dredged south of Snodland. In conclusion, it is Thornhill's view that by Romano-British times, as tides progressively advanced up the Medway Valley, wayfarers were forced to use the Snodland rocks crossing rather than the lower Holborough crossing.

Even though Belloc's argument concludes that it is less likely that prehistoric travellers crossed at Aylesford, it is interesting to note the number of post-Ice Age archaeological finds in the upper Medway Valley in line with Wrotham and Blue Bell Hill. These finds include 'the largest concentration of Mesolithic' flints at Addington,[44] an assemblage of early Mesolithic tools found at Ditton (Clark, 1932, pp. 70–71)[45] situated 1 mile west of Aylesford, and axes made from fine-grained rock heads, which Ashbee describes as 'an integral feature of our Neolithic', found at New Hythe.[46] This certainly suggests that within a broad 6-mile line passing through the Aylesford area between Coldrum and Kit's Coty, there is ample evidence of prehistoric human activity.

Moreover, the Neolithic burial chambers at Addington and the Chestnuts are on a direct line and midway between Wrotham and Aylesford. These long barrows have revealed a number of Neolithic finds, including potsherds.[47] Later, important Bronze Age finds were made at burial sites to the north-west of Aylesford church. Three burial cists, made of tufa and sandstone, contained a number of bronze items, including a bronze bound bucket and an imported Italian jug and pan.[48]

Gold work in the form of bracelets was also found at Aylesford, 'enclosed in a box which was alleged to have been thrown into the river'.[49] Paul Ashbee suggests that from Neolithic times onwards there are hints of Kent 'having an especial role in the country's trading activities'.[50] Champion notes the pre-historic sources of copper and tin found in the Kent area and suggests that trading links with western England amongst other places may have existed.

South-eastern England has no native source of copper or tin, so all the metalwork found there must be made from imported materials. The copper may have come from western England, Wales or Ireland, or possibly from sources on the Continent.[51]

This, of course, fits with, but does not necessarily support, Grant Allen's tin road theory, which many of the pilgrimist writers give particular credence too.[52] Given all of the above arguments, it is less inconceivable than Belloc's argument that prehistoric travellers crossed the river as high as the Aylesford area.

Legend, according to Francis Watt, writing about the Medway megaliths in 1917, has it that: 'an avenue lined with those mammoth blocks ran from Kits Coty House to Coldrum; it led to a crude temple or ancient place of burial. Some have professed to trace this avenue through the Medway which runs by Aylesford.'[53]

If such a line of stones once marked an avenue across the Medway Gap, it is also interesting to note that the Coldrum stones and Kit's Coty House stand at the same height above sea level on either side of the Medway Gap. As regards the stones' respective heights, the facts cannot be disputed and both megaliths are situated at a height of 95 metres above present sea level, at a distance of 6 miles apart on either side of the Medway Gap. Perhaps an avenue of stones stretching across the valley is somewhat more fanciful. William Coles Finch also makes reference to an authority, James Fergusson, DCL, FCS, who described an avenue of stones on the east bank of the Medway Valley.[54] Fergusson was referring to a much shorter avenue, approximately ¾ mile in length, at the rear of Kit's Coty and Little Kit's Coty, running from Spring Farm to Hale Farm, and states: 'there exists, or existed, a line of great stones, extending from a place called Spring Farm, in a north easterly direction, for a distance of three quarters of a mile to another spot known as Hale Farm, passing through Tollington, where the greater number of stones are now found.'[55]

Fergusson also refers to the fact that an elderly stonemason recounted to him how he had been employed in his youth to utilise many of the stones and pointed out the position of those he remembered. Therefore, it is less surprising that Coles Finch informed his readers in 1925 that from his research 'the three quarters of a mile of great stone is no more'. Christopher John Wright, in his *Guide to the Pilgrims' Way*, also mentions the tradition of an avenue of stones that stretched between the Coldrum Stones to Kit's Coty House. However, rather than at Aylesford, he suggests that the 'river crossing at Snodland would be the natural route between the two'.[56]

Belloc's favoured crossing point is at Snodland, which has also given up
a number of prehistoric archaeological finds within the vicinity, including
Neolithic pottery.[57] And Goodsall notes 'the many finds on both banks prove
the importance of the area in Roman times'.[58] Belloc suggested that the river
bed at Snodland may have been artificially hardened to create a causeway.
However, Goodsall states at this spot there is a natural outcrop of greensand
(Kentish Ragstone) which has defied all dredging operations in the past.[59]
Nevertheless, it has also been suggested that the 'causeway is a feature in the
river bed known as the "Snodland Rocks" – a bar of iron-cemented con-
glomerate, with large and small flints and pebbly material visible at low tide'.[60]

In 2005, the BBC South East presenter, Kaddy Lee-Preston, with the help
of the Kent Fire Service, waded across the River Medway at Snodland. The
BBC had consulted local Snodland historian Andrew Ashbee, who advised
the filmmakers as to the exact location of the hard base and the fact that it
could be crossed at low tide. In 2009 the author was introduced by Andrew
Ashbee to Robert Coomber, a local Snodland resident and volunteer worker
at the Snodland Museum. He described how, as a young man in the late 1940s,
he had crossed the River Medway on foot to retrieve a pigeon he had shot,
which fell on to the far bank. Mr Coomber crossed at a point at TQ 714615,
situated slightly south of the Horseshoe Reach and adjacent to Brookland
Lake, with Burham marshes on the opposite bank. He described the river
bed's surface as consisting of fist-sized rocks that provided for a secure and
firm passage underfoot.[61]

Nigel Nicholson's article in *Current Archaeology* 157 makes the point that it is
now thought that the Roman army, led by Aulus Plautius, defeated the British
tribes on the west bank of the Medway in AD 43. He suggests that Vespasian led
his legion of 5000 armoured men across the river at Snodland. He also states
that the army used the North Kent coastal plain, the North Downs and also
the Pilgrims' Way as routes from the Kent coast through to the Medway.

Given that there is only a marginal difference in distance between the
Coldrum Stones and Kit's Coty, using either the Snodland crossing or the
Aylesford crossing, combined with the evidence of human activity in the
region, it is just as likely that prehistoric travellers crossed at both Snodland
and Aylesford. Moreover, these crossing points may well have changed due to
seasonal variations in the weather in addition to changes over longer periods
of time, as discussed above.

Belloc also argues that the existence of churches on either side of the
Snodland crossing is a positive factor. This surely is hardly relevant, as Belloc
is considering the development of a prehistoric route and not a medieval
crossing. Even if he could argue that churches signify religious sites of a
much earlier date, he does not suggest this nor considers this even relevant

44 Burham church, east side of Snodland Crossing

to an earlier society. If anything, the proximity of the churches so close to one another, on either side of the river at Snodland, suggests that crossing in the medieval period was not an everyday task. Anyway, it would appear that key sites (i.e. the megaliths), which may have held some prehistoric spiritual significance, are situated at the western and eastern periphery of the Medway Gap. Ivan Margary picks up on this point and states that Belloc seems ultimately 'too much swayed by the presence of religious buildings quite unconnected with prehistoric considerations'.[62] Nevertheless, the Norman churches at Snodland and Burham may have held some significance for medieval pilgrims.

Belloc also argues that the Horseshoe Reach at Snodland is favoured because it is the upper limit of where the sea town (Rochester) has jurisdiction over the lower Medway. He suggests that this is always the traditional crossing point of a river. Again, this factor is of no relevance to the prehistoric traveller and, as such, does not apply.

Finally, manorial records for the manor of the Bishop of Rochester show that on 8 April 1720, John May 'lately obstructed and diverted the King's Highway in a field called the twelve acres leading from Snodland to Gravesend'.[63] Whilst it is beyond the scope of this work to suggest that a direct route existed between Snodland and Gravesend that could have been used by medieval travellers, it is known that Hasted refers to a ferry between Essex and Lillechurch at Higham, near Gravesend, which he describes as being used up until the Dissolution.[64]

45 Burham Church –
belfrywheel

After Snodland, Lower Halling is the next lowest crossing point considered by Belloc apart from Cuxton. Belloc suggests that at Halling the alluvial
soil is less broad than at Snodland and 'no clay intervenes between the chalk
and gravel' and as such 'the primitive traveller would have dry land all the
way down to the river'.[65] Nevertheless, Belloc discounts Halling in favour
of Snodland, his reason being that the spur known as the Holborough knob,
which jutted out from the chalk escarpment into the valley, left Snodland on
the dryer south side of the spur and Halling on the north side of the spur.
Today, much of the Holborough knob has been cut back through quarrying.
As a result of this quarrying, the hillside now lines up with the general curve
of the west side of the chalk escarpment rather than jutting out toward the
river bank. The previous position of the Holborough knob therefore leads
Belloc to argue that 'in such a conformation only the southern bank alone
would have any chance of drying'.[66] However, this is somewhat contradictory
as Belloc already has testified to the lack of clay between the chalk escarpment and the gravel of the river, making for dryer ground underfoot on the
approach to Halling.

The lack of antiquities found at Halling compared with what Belloc describes as numerous finds at Snodland is for him another factor. Belloc also argues that the Snodland crossing had a ford, whereas the river bed at Halling is soft and a ferry-crossing would need to be undertaken. Nevertheless, at the time of writing he did not have the benefit of Patrick Thornhill's research in light of the borings undertaken at Snodland and Halling.

The notes of Rev. Henry Dampier Phelps, Rector of Snodland 1804–65, written in the 1840s, suggest both road access and a river crossing at Halling, when he wrote:

Many other proofs of the Romans having a Station in this Parish still remain; especially one of their Roads, which now forms our Northern Boundary and runs in a line from the Hills to the River where they crossed and where the Road is again found pointing directly up from the River.★ … [Corresponding footnote:] In digging on the Wouldham side, to make a sheep wash, it was found that the Bank of the River had been paved to admit of a ferry and facilitate crossing at low water.[67]

Phelps' argument for a crossing at Halling, served as it was by a Roman road, is also supported by reference to a map drawn by A.F. Bowker CE, FRGS, entitled 'Malling and its Valley', published in the Rev. C.F. Fielding's *Memories of Malling and its Valley*. This shows a straight road running due east from Chapel House, following the line of the parish boundary to the river, then continuing in exactly the same line on the east bank and joining up with the Rochester Road, leading to Kit's Coty.

Edward Hasted (1798) also makes reference to a river crossing at lower Halling, and states:

In the northern part of the parish next to Lower Halling, is the hamlet of Holborough, usually called Hoborow, no doubt for Old Borough, a name implying the antiquity of this place. Many are inclined to believe, that the usual passage across the river in the time of the Romans, was from hence to Scarborough on the opposite shore.[68]

The lowest crossing point Belloc considers is Cuxton, which he discounts despite acknowledging that the ancient trackway continues north along the side of the chalk downs on either side of the river and would appear to converge towards a crossing point at Cuxton, which would necessitate a ferry (see map above). Moreover Belloc states 'as a constant tradition maintains, the crossing of the river by pilgrims was common'.[69] Notwithstanding this, Belloc is judging this from the viewpoint of prehistoric travellers and argues that to continue downstream until the Cuxton crossing 'would add five or six miles to his journey'.[70] He adds that the bottom is soft mud, the width of the river is considerable, the tidal current strong and of all the points at which the river might have been crossed, it is the most distant from the direct line'.[71]

Captain E. Renouard James, the Ordnance Survey officer, who was a significant figure in the development of pilgrimist theory, states in his published *Notes on the Pilgrims' Way* that he believed Cuxton to be the point where pilgrims crossed the Medway, unless they chose to go on to Rochester. The author has assumed that Captain E.R. James comes down in favour of Cuxton because he tracked the course of a North Downs trackway along the west bank of the Medway, beyond North Halling, towards Cuxton. He does not say in his notes whether medieval travellers would have crossed the river at Cuxton by ford or ferry, but given Thornhill's conclusions with regard to the changing state of the valley floor since prehistoric times, it would appear that the lower crossings should not be discounted for prehistoric travellers. Moreover, Ivan Margary, whilst concluding that 'it would be misleading to point to any one spot as "the crossing"', does however argue that Belloc did not give sufficient consideration to a Cuxton crossing, when he states:

> But why then should the terrace-way continue north? The reason may well be this. Below Halling, near Holborough, the river widens into a tidal estuary, though sheltered, and with firm ground right down to the water on both banks, especially near Cuxton and Borstal. If a raft or boat had to be used in any case, it might well be easier to use this where firm ground gave good landings on either bank, even if this involved a somewhat longer water crossing.[72]

Whilst it is known that the Romans established a bridge at Rochester, what is not known is if the bridge was constantly maintained following the Roman occupation. A bridge existed in the thirteenth century in the form of a wooden structure and, according to Stow's *Annales* (1631), this entirely collapsed due to severe weather in the winter of 1281.[73] Crossing the Medway at Rochester was not without its dangers, as Diana Webb informs us: 'but pilgrims were among those who from time to time were drowned crossing the Medway by ferry when the bridge was broken, which happened no fewer than nineteen times between 1277 and 1381.'[74]

In 1387 the first stone bridge was built, situated 100 yards upstream from the original Roman bridge. The dangerous state of the old Rochester bridge, prior to the construction of the new bridge at the end of the fourteenth century, may well have been another determining factor for many in opting for the crossing upstream and then following the North Downs trackway as their chosen route to Canterbury or Dover. However, Sean Jennet suggests that in winter months the upstream crossings may have proved the more difficult and this could have influenced medieval travellers (Group B) to continue the few additional miles on into Rochester to use the bridge.

We have to remember that for the first 50 years of pilgrimage to Canterbury the month of December was the prime occasion of the veneration of the saint. In that month it was always possible that after days of rain or snow the river would be swollen and perilous, the valley flooded and the ferry boats untempting. At Rochester, however, there was a bridge, and there a man might cross the Medway in safety.[75]

Given the importance of Boxley abbey, it is likely that some pilgrims coming from the London direction may have chosen to leave the Watling Street route after crossing the Medway at Rochester Bridge. Pilgrims would have then followed the terrace-way track, today known as both the Burham Road and the Pilgrims' Way, to Kit's Coty and on to Boxley abbey, which lies on the eastern fringe of the Medway Gap and within close proximity to the North Downs trackway. Boxley abbey was founded in 1146 and remained a promi-nent Cistercian monastery until the Dissolution. The abbey became a case of notoriety at the time of the Reformation when the Rood of Grace and the figure of St Rumbold, which took on life-like qualities when presented with offerings by pilgrims, were exposed as mere mechanical tricks operated by the monks. William Coles Finch, in *In Kentish Pilgrims Land*, informs his readers that 'no pilgrim of medieval days would leave the Abbey unvisited'.[76]

Having examined all the Medway river crossings it would appear that there is a strong case for travellers in Group B, approaching the Medway Gap from the west of England and south of London, to have used the crossings upstream, such as at Aylesford, Snodland or Halling. In view of the popularity of Boxley abbey as a pilgrimage destination, there is also reason to accept that some in Group A may have crossed at Rochester Bridge or Cuxton and picked up the trackways along the east bank of the Medway to Kit's Coty.

8

Population and Pilgrimage

The Scale of Long-Distance Pilgrimage

An assessment needs to be made of the actual numbers of the population eligible to undertake an extended pilgrimage in the Middle
Ages. By working backwards from recorded offerings made at
Becket's shrine, combined with working forward from Domesday statistics,
taking account of geographic location and social class, a much more realistic
estimate of the numbers of medieval travellers that may have chosen to use
the North Downs trackways can be arrived at.

Much of the criticism of pilgrimist theory with regard to the use of the
North Downs trackways as a route of medieval pilgrimage is aimed at what
is probably fair to describe as the exaggerated claims of antiquarians writing
in the nineteenth century regarding the numbers undertaking the journey.
Nevertheless, despite such criticism, these claims have been subject to little
in-depth scrutiny. By assessing the scale of offerings at Becket's shrine, as well
as using Domesday population statistics, it can be argued that the scale of
extended pilgrimage to Canterbury was far less than many imagine. As such,
not only could the Pilgrims' Way sustain the relative low levels of medieval
pilgrimage but, for many travellers from the west of the country, the route
also presented an attractive option in comparison with the decaying, ill-main-
tained and risk-laden Roman road network.

Pilgrimist Exaggerations

Elliston-Erwood was one of the first critics to suggest the likelihood of there
having been far fewer pilgrims than had been claimed by pilgrimist writers.

In 1925 he wrote that 'the mediaeval religious pilgrimage is a matter that has been grossly exaggerated in the past'.[1] His conclusions were based upon his application of a quantative assessment of the recorded offerings made at Becket's shrine.

To this end, Elliston-Erwood divided the published accounts of offerings to Beckett's shrines by his own suggested average offering of 4 shillings per pilgrim. In so doing he arrived at a figure of 1000 pilgrims per year. He then estimated across the year and arrived at an average of two pilgrims a day, outside of the great festivals. As Elliston-Erwood states: 'Thus pilgrimage is reduced to more reasonable dimensions. Chaucer's pilgrims become more illuminating; and the effect of such travellers on a country road becomes negligible.'[2]

For dissenters from the view that the trackway was used by pilgrims, there is an array of targets. As the pilgrimists' claims regarding the numbers using the way increased, so did the ease by which their statements became open to criticism. It is not too difficult to see how the claims of some pilgrimists appear to build upon one another over time.

E.G. Crump, a staunch critic of the pilgrimist tradition, noted that in the early nineteenth century Manning and Bray claimed that the route was used only by pilgrims from the west. They did not enumerate further about the scale of pilgrimage. Crump's essay, published in June 1936 shortly after his death, was steered through to publication on his behalf by Charles Johnson. He asserts his own scepticism about the Pilgrims' Way from the outset and explains to the reader that for some 40 years he had 'thoroughly disliked the Pilgrims' Way' and 'believed it to a be a fond thing grounded upon no uncertain warranty of history, and so intrinsically absurd that it was not worth criticism'.[3] In fact, Crump was only stirred into writing about the Pilgrims' Way in reaction to an article that had been published the previous year in *History* (June 1935) by Dr Peter Brieger, who stated:

> The religious spirit of the Middle Ages thronged the roads with pilgrims on their way to Rome and the Holy Land. Even more numerous were those who undertook pilgrimages to Holy Places in England itself. The most celebrated of these was the shrine of St Thomas of Canterbury, and the Pilgrims' Way between Winchester and Canterbury was in consequence by far the best road in England.[4]

Crump lays out in chronological order what he believes are the exaggerated claims of the pilgrimists and demonstrates how these claims compound over time. He points out that Edward Brayley, in his *Topographical History of Surrey* Volume V of 1850, upon discovering a section of the Way in the parish of Albury, informs his readers that 'the Pilgrims' Way, which led from the city of

46 Archbishop Juxon's coat of arms, Christ Church Gate, Butter Market

Winchester to Canterbury crosses this parish, and is said to have been *much used* in former times' (author's emphasis).[5]

By 1871 Captain E.R. James, the Ordnance Survey officer responsible for denoting stretches of trackway as the Pilgrims' Way, was describing the route as one that had been 'frequented by crowds of pilgrims'.[6] In his *Notes on the Pilgrims Way in West Surrey*, Captain James stated that pilgrims using the trackway 'came, doubtless, the greatest numbers from the royal and ecclesiastical city of Winchester, where they assembled from Salisbury and all parts of western England, and thence followed the old Roman road to Farnham'.[7]

Despite omitting Captain James' contribution, in his list of Victorian descriptions of ever-growing numbers of medieval pilgrims using the North Downs trackway, Crump quotes from a letter by someone he describes as a true believer, published in *Notes and Queries*, dated 21 September 1850, who describes 'a vast influx of pilgrims' as using the road. According to the author of the letter, pilgrims started their pilgrimage to Becket's shrine from its true commencement at Otford.

Crump goes on to note that by 1893 Julia Cartwright was referring to 'thousands of pilgrims'. In fact, Cartwright states in her opening chapter that: 'this route it is, which, trodden by thousands of pilgrims during the next three centuries, may still be clearly defined through the greater part of its course, and which in Surrey and Kent bears the historic name of the Pilgrims' Way.'[8]

Crump reminds us that, nine years following the publication of *The Pilgrims' Way from Winchester to Canterbury*, Hilaire Belloc's *The Old Road* describes how 'hordes of international pilgrims' streamed towards Becket's shrine. Belloc lists their places of origin as the south-western peninsula of England, Brittany, the Asturias and the western ports from Vigo to Lisbon, and says 'all these sent their hordes to converge on Winchester and thence to find their way to Canterbury'.[9]

By 1925 William Coles Finch, in his *In Kentish Pilgrim Land*, informs his readership, based upon a reference by A.S. Lamprey in a *Guide to Maidstone*, that: 'Along that mysterious road known as the Pilgrims' Way travelled as many as a hundred thousand pilgrims a year to the shrine of Thomas a Becket.'[10]

It's of little surprise, therefore, that the pilgrimist writers came under attack from the likes of Crump, Elliston-Erwood, Captain W.H. Knocker and Wilfrid Hooper. Perhaps the biggest mistake made by the pilgrimists is that they over egged the pudding. Hooper argued, in an article published in the *Surrey Archaeological Collections* Volume 44 in 1936, that writers like Belloc and Cartwright accepted the 'pilgrimist theory as an established historical fact'. But, more importantly, he notes that: 'In their train have followed the host of guide-books and popular writers who have expanded and embellished ad libitum as fancy prompted.'[11]

A fundamental problem exists, with regard to much of the criticism of the pilgrimist writers, in that it has been undertaken with little analysis of the actual numbers that would have engaged in medieval pilgrimage. Any consideration of the scale of pilgrimage needs to be undertaken with an understanding of the population, in terms of people's position within the medieval social hierarchy, in as much as how this affected an individual's right to freedom of travel beyond their own manor. Such analysis could provide a better understanding of the numbers that may have used a particular route, but also needs to take into consideration demographic trends during the period of medieval pilgrimage.

Ronald C. Finucane noted that we know very little about the ordinary person and pilgrimage for the reason that little was actually recorded. As Diana Webb states:

> Among the various types of documentation thus created, the records of offerings at shrines, which naturally survive most often from the larger churches, occupy one extreme of objectivity. Although these are obviously of the greatest value, not least in making possible some idea of the popularity of shrines and alters over a period of time, the ordinary pilgrim as an individual does not feature in them; his penny or his candle is subsumed in the mass.[12]

Nevertheless there is evidence to suggest substantial numbers of pilgrims did journey to Canterbury between the twelfth and sixteenth centuries. Reference to the scale of pilgrimage is mentioned in one of the Paston letters, believed to be written in the year after the fifth jubilee of Becket's translation. In a letter dated 28 September 1471, Sir John Paston states: 'As ffor tydyngs, the Kyng and the Qwyen, and moche other pepell, ar ryden and good to Canterbery. Nevyr so moche pepie seyn in Pylgrymage hertofor or at ones, as men seye.'[13]

Quantative Assessment based on Offerings at the Shrine

One method of quantifying the numerical scale of pilgrimage to Canterbury is to examine the shrine accounts of offerings made by pilgrims at the four stations associated with the cult of St Thomas. This work was undertaken by Ben Nilson, who studied the Canterbury Cathedral Priory's receipts for the years when the treasurers' accounts were maintained between 1198/9 and 1384/5. Thereafter prior's accounts survive but these cover only 18 years between 1396/7 and 1473/4. A final set of sacrist's accounts cover the year for 1531/2.[14]

Taking Nilson's figures for shrine offerings, the author has divided these by the minimum (2*d*) and maximum (4*s*) offerings per person as referred to by Elliston-Erwood.[15] From this we find that the highest number of pilgrims could have been as high as 128,520 in the year of the 1220 jubilee, when the four stations received £1071 0*s* 2*d*, assuming an average offering as low as 2*d* per pilgrim across all shrines, including the main shrine, the martyrdom, the corona and the tomb – or as low as 5355 pilgrims, assuming an average offering as high as 4*s* per pilgrim. Applying this method to other years, where the total offerings to all the shrines were recorded, we can estimate a possible maximum or minimum range for the numbers of pilgrims.

If the year of the translation of Becket's relics (1220) represented the numerical highpoint, then the year of 1200/1 was another similarly good year in terms of offerings, when the total received at the three stations (the shrine was not established until the translation) amounted to £537. Therefore the highest number of pilgrims could have been 64,440 pilgrims, assuming an average of 2*d* per pilgrim, or as few as 2685, assuming an average of 4*s* per pilgrim.

By 1269/70 offerings received at the four stations had fallen to £151 6*s*. As such, the average number of pilgrims decreases to a maximum of 18,156, offering 2*d* per pilgrim, or a minimum of 756 pilgrims, offering 4*s* per pilgrim. By the year of the fourth jubilee in 1420 offerings at the four stations appear to have returned to levels similar to 1200. As such, this equates to a maximum figure of 68,400 or a minimum of 2850.

According to Nilson's research, only the sacrist's account for 1531/32 offers any record of offerings to St Thomas near to the time of the Dissolution. The total to the various alters in the church of £13 13*s* 3*d* suggests a maximum of 1639 or a minimum of 68 pilgrims per year.

The above figures offer a means of quantifying the scale of pilgrimage to Becket's shrine for certain years between 1198/9 and 1531/2. However, such a broad brush approach does not tell us where these pilgrims came from, nor does it inform us of their social background. Both of these questions are relevant to any enquiry regarding the numbers of medieval pilgrims that may have taken the ancient trackway as their chosen route to Canterbury.

Social position within a feudal society is important. It is doubtful that large sections of the population would have had the freedom to make an extended pilgrimage. It was not only slaves that would have had their freedom of movement restricted. Large numbers of villeins and cottagers were tied to the manor due to their position in the feudal social hierarchy.[16] The question of social position may also offer clues as to the size of average offerings over time. The change in the social composition of pilgrims is a point that has been noted by some commentators and may well reflect changes in population size and subsequent pressures on the rigidities of feudalism by the end of the fourteenth century. Sumption suggests that 'the declining social status of pilgrims was as a general phenomenon of the fourteenth and fifteenth centuries, and its immediate effect was to reduce the income from offerings while increasing the number of visitors who needed free food and board'.[17]

It is well documented that at various times legislation was enacted with a view to restricting who could leave the land. Moreover, such legislation would often refer directly to those leaving the manor for the purpose of undertaking pilgrimage. Diana Webb, referring to legislation enacted in 1388–89, notes in *Pilgrimage in Medieval England* that: 'The statute includes the stipulation that all of them that go in pilgrimage as beggars and be able to travail, it shall be done as Servants and Labourers, if they have no Letters testimonial of their pilgrimage.'[18]

The extent to which pilgrimage undertaken by the lower classes was perceived as threatening to the social order was reflected in a directive to the sheriffs of London in 1473, which forbade people from undertaking pilgrimage if they could not perform it without alms. As Webb suggests, the 'thrust, as before was ostensibly against mendicancy and not against pilgrimage undertaken by respectable people with money in their purse'.[19]

An Alternative Approach to Calculating Pilgrim Numbers

Using the Domesday records we can make an assessment of the size of the population that would have been eligible to undertake an extended medieval pilgrimage. Domesday also allows us to estimate the size of the population and its geographic location. This alternative approach has been undertaken with particular reference to counties situated to the west of the country and south of London, i.e. locations from which travellers may have chosen to use the Pilgrims' Way as a pilgrimage route to Canterbury. It should be noted at the outset that the author is fully aware of the well-known pitfalls in using Domesday data and in making the various, often heroic, assumptions that are required. All the steps in the calculations are described in detail for the reader to follow.

In undertaking this exercise, the author has overestimated by inclusion wherever there is doubt, so as to increase the numbers of potential travellers rather than limit numbers. This has been done because the exercise is aimed at demonstrating that far fewer numbers of the population were able to undertake pilgrimage than may have been previously assumed.

For this reason, the whole of the following nine counties have been included, as follows: Cornwall, Devon, Dorset, Hampshire, Kent, Somerset, Surrey, Sussex and Wiltshire. In reality, simply due to proximity and location, it would not have been practical for the populations of large geographic areas in some of these counties to have accessed the Pilgrims' Way.

Furthermore, adjustments need to be made to the Domesday population figures as Domesday does not provide a census of the population in 1086. As Robert Bartlett points out: 'Domesday Book was not intended as a population census. It lists a rural population of 268,863 individuals, but that is certainly not the population of England in 1086, and in order to obtain that figure we have to make some assumptions about what Domesday leaves out.'[20]

The total recorded rural population of Domesday England is 268,863, which, as H.C. Darby suggests, 'we are left to suppose that each recorded man was the head of a household'.[21] By using a multiplier, derived through evidence from the thirteenth century that suggests a peasant household of 4.7 persons, Bartlett offers a figure for the total rural Domesday population of 1.26 million. The multiplier applied in this exercise is the slightly higher conventional one of 5, as suggested by H.C. Darby's research.[22]

Account should also be taken of what H.C. Darby suggests is the Domesday exclusion of the northernmost counties. In addition, Bartlett notes the exclusion of the urban populations, including Winchester and London, the secular aristocracy and their dependents, as well as ecclesiastics and their servants. This brings a total population for Domesday England to 1.5 million. This alternative approach takes account of these adjustments below.

A further adjustment also needs to made to allow for a possible unreported number of sub-tenants and landless persons, which could account for a further 750,000 people. This brings Bartlet's estimate of England's Domesday population to an approximate total of 2.25 million.

It has been estimated that by 1230 the population had increased to 5.8 million, which represents an increase of 156 per cent. However, in the aftermath of the Black Death it is believed that the total population may have decreased to 3.5 million. These changes in population over time should be borne in mind when using Domesday data for determining the size of the population. However, within the scope of this present calculation it is felt that the output figures derived from the 1086 data remain indicative of the scale of pilgrimage, but there is no reason why the final numbers should not be weighted to reflect the above variation in population over time.

Applying Darby's multiplier of 5 to the Domesday population total of 89,594 for the nine counties, we arrive at a rural population of nearly half a million.[23]

Domesday population in the nine counties from which medieval travellers may have accessed the Pilgrims' Way									
Villeins	X 5***	S-holders	X 5	Slaves	X 5	Ancillary	X 5	Freemen*	X 5
40517	202585	28742	143710	13274	66370	8	40	27	135
Free men**	X 5	Priests		Cottagers	X 5	Burgesses	X 5	Other	X 5
0	0	31		2206	11030	2592	12960	2197	10985
								Total population	X 5***
								89594	447846

*   Freemen or sokemen, males with socage

**   Free men (freedmen) or *liberi homine* – all base data derived from Palmer, J. et al., Electronic Edition of Domesday Book: Translation, Databases and Scholarly Commentary, 1086 (computer file).

***   Multiplier of 5 applied to Domesday recorded heads of households to estimate population numbers; see H.C. Darby – excluding priests

This total of 447,846 individuals is the sum of the nine Domesday social groups and is divided between villagers/villeins 202,585 (45 per cent); smallholders 143,710 (32 per cent); slaves 66,370 (15 per cent); ancillary 40 (0 per cent); freemen 135 (1 per cent); priests 31 (0 per cent); cottagers 11,030 (2 per cent); burgesses 12,960 (3 per cent); and others 10,985 (2 per cent).

A number of social groups can be discounted from those that would have been eligible to leave the manor to go on pilgrimage, such as slaves and cottagers or cottars. It is generally regarded that cottars formed one of the lowest groups within the peasantry and, as such, were considered below most of the villeiny in terms of social status. Of the other six social groups from the remaining seven, it has been assumed that most, i.e. smallholders, ancillaries, burgesses, freemen, priests and others, would have been free to choose to go on pilgrimage. The final and largest social group, the villeins or villeinage, were the least likely to be free to leave the manor. This group comprised 45 per cent of the Domesday population.

Jusserand states that:

> The villein who, without special licence, left his master's domain, only entered the common life again after putting himself at his mercy, or, which was less hard, after having passed a year and a day in a free town without leaving it and without the lord having thought of interrupting the prescription.[24]

Bartlett argues that the compulsory provision of labour services to the lord was one of the factors that determined the features of villeinage, when he suggests:

> One of the most obvious distinctions amongst the peasant tenantry was between those who had to march off to work on the lord's farm for two or three days a week and those who did not. Although labour services in themselves, particularly the obligation to help with the ploughing and harvesting, did not imply servile status, the heavy burden of weekly work, and in particular the uncertainty of services required, could be taken as a defining feature of villeinage.[25]

Therefore, if one concludes that 'most villeins do not travel more than a few miles from their manor, on account of their bond to their lord, but freeman can — and do — travel much further afield', then it would not be unreasonable to discount a large proportion of villeins from those that would be eligible to undertake pilgrimage.[26] As Jusserand noted, it was 'escaped peasants that brought the most numerous recruits to the wandering class'.[27] Moreover, tensions within English feudal society, demonstrated by events such as the Peasant's Revolt, were reflected in the introduction of legislation such as the 1376 prohibition on the movement of individuals out of a man's own district.[28]

Some recent approaches to understanding medieval society have looked beyond the feudal structure of the manor. Schofield remarks that: 'Historians now look for and find peasants in contexts beyond the manor and villages, in markets, in country courts, in military levies, or on pilgrimage.'[29]

Furthermore, Sumption, commenting on the bequests made by pilgrims to the four Canterbury jubilees in the late Middle Ages, noted that they 'drew large crowds of pilgrims but the great and wealthy stayed away' and states that: 'declining social status of pilgrims was a general phenomenon of the fourteenth and fifteenth centuries, and its immediate effect was to reduce the income from offerings while increasing the number of visitors who needed free food and board.'[30]

In consideration of the arguments that peasants could be found in contexts beyond the manor, the author has only discounted two-thirds of the population that fall within the category of villein from being eligible to undertake pilgrimage, but has included one-third, or 68,528 villeins. Bartlett suggests that: (i) based upon H.C. Darby's estimate, 120,000 should be added to the Domesday population to take account of the urban population; (ii) together with a further 66,000 to account for the secular aristocracy and their household dependents; and (iii) 50,000 to account for ecclesiastics and their servants.[31] This is an additional 236,000 over and above the total Domesday rural population. Bartlett therefore adjusts the Domesday total by 18.7 per cent.

The author has not included Darby's adjustment of 33,000 for the north-ernmost counties within the 18.7 per cent. All of these groups are included within the eligible pilgrimage category.

Therefore, if we add Bartlett's adjustment of 18.7 per cent proportionately to the population for the nine southern and western counties of England of 447,846, i.e. those that could have accessed the North Downs ancient track-ways, we arrive at a total of 531,593. From this we need to subtract 135,057 to account for two-thirds of those that fall within the social group of villeins that would be least likely to be eligible to travel away from the manor on pilgrimage. This gives a population eligible to undertake pilgrimage from the nine southern and western counties of nearly 400,000. From this we also need to discount cottagers and slaves, which account for 77,400, which reduces the number eligible to travel on pilgrimage to roughly 320,000.

It has been argued by Postan that up to one-third of the total population, amounting to 750,000, was landless and therefore excluded from Domesday. In effect, Bartlett adds 59.5 per cent to the Domesday rural population total of 1.26 million to account for this, another 266,468.[32] We have to decide whether or not those that fall within the category of landless would have been eligible to undertake pilgrimage. For the benefit of doubt, the author has included half of this group (133,234) as eligible to undertake pilgrimage. This brings the total number from the population eligible to undertake pilgrimage from the nine counties of southern and western England in the region of 450,000.

Number of people from the population of the nine southern and western counties likely to commence pilgrimage to Canterbury on any single day				
Those eligible to travel from southern and western west counties	450,000	450,000	450,000	450,000
Those within age range for pilgrimage i.e. between 14 and 65 = 55% pop'*	247,500	247,500	247,500	247,500
Those that choose to go on pilgrimage to Canterbury in lifetime (50%, 30%, 20 %, or 10% of population)	123,750 (50%)	74,250 (30%)	49,500 (20%)	24,750 (10%)
Those that choose that year in which to travel (divide by 29)**	4267	2560	1707	853
Those that commence pilgrimage on any single day in that year (182)***	23	14	9	5

*   Based upon 1377 poll tax returns that show 40 per cent of the population was 13 years of age or less and 5 per cent was over 65 (Hatcher, *Plague Population*, from Mortimer, Ian, 2009)

**   Assumes one extended pilgrimage taken during an average 29 available years to travel based on Crude Expectation Ages for those reaching 15 years of age (Russell, Josiah Cox, *British Medieval Population*, University of New Mexico, 1948, p. 176)

★★★   Assumes choice to commence pilgrimage on any one day across six months (182 days)
of the year. If commencement day was evenly distributed across whole year (365 days) then
average daily numbers would reduce to: 12, 7, 5 or 3 respectively

Therefore, a figure in the region of 450,000 represents the total number of
the population eligible to travel on pilgrimage from the nine counties to the
south and west of London. From this total we need to discount those that
would have been too young or too old to undertake an extended pilgrimage, assuming that only during a proportion of an individual's lifespan would
they be within an age range to travel. To this end, the author has included 55
per cent of the population that was between 14 and 65 years of age, derived
from Hatcher's research on the 1377 poll tax returns.[33] Account also needs to
be taken of the number of those that would have chosen to take a pilgrimage
in their own lifetime. The author has applied factors representing between
50 per cent and 10 per cent of those eligible to travel as a range of those that
would have chosen to undertake pilgrimage in their lifetime. We must also
consider that each individual would only undertake a pilgrimage once in
their lifetime rather than in each year. Therefore, the author has divided the
number of those eligible to undertake an extended pilgrimage by Russell's
average lifespan for those reaching the age of 15.[34] As such, the total has been
divided by 29.

Finally, it has been assumed that about half of the days within the year
would provide suitable weather conditions to undertake an extended pilgrimage. As such, based upon the above loose assumptions when applied
to the Domesday population, it can be seen that if pilgrimage was undertaken by 50 per cent of the eligible population then on any one day across
six months of the year one could expect to see 23 pilgrims commencing a
journey using the North Downs trackways. If only 10 per cent of the eligible population from the nine southern and western counties undertook
a pilgrimage to Canterbury, then on any one day across six months of the
year, one could expect to see five pilgrims commencing a journey using the
North Downs trackways.

However, given that up until 1220 the period of major pilgrimage coincided
with 29 December, the date of Beckett's martyrdom, until the translation of
Becket's relics, we know that pilgrimage was also undertaken in the winter
months. As such, the average daily number of pilgrims commencing pilgrimage
could be reduced further still if their numbers are spread across the whole year.

This model does not allow for overseas pilgrims entering the country at
Southampton and using the Pilgrims' Way as a route to Canterbury, rather
than sailing to one of the Kent sea ports. It is beyond the scope of this exercise
to evaluate the number of overseas' pilgrims and their reasons for using the

Pilgrims' Way, although it can be seen that even if they doubled the traffic, the numbers would still remain relatively small.

The above model overestimates numbers as it is based on the assumption that all those undertaking pilgrimage to Canterbury from the nine southern and western counties found the North Downs trackways to be the most suitable route, which would not have been the case for large geographic areas of these counties. Once consideration is given to the size of and restrictions of movement pertaining to the medieval population, it can be seen that the number of pilgrims travelling along the North Downs trackways would have been very small – much smaller than the exaggerated claims made by the pilgrimists.

Perhaps there is less reason to suppose that the Pilgrims' Way could not have served as a viable route, used by medieval travellers as their chosen route to Canterbury. It can be argued that whilst detractors of the way as a pilgrimage route have been eager to point to the exaggerated claims made by Victorian and Edwardian pilgrimists, they have been less inclined to offer any quantitative assessment of the limited scale of mass pilgrimage overall. If this is undertaken, the use of the North Downs trackways should be reconsidered within the context of much lower levels of pilgrimage traffic. Given this reassessment of numbers, it can be argued that the way could easily have sustained the limited numbers of pilgrims travelling from the west.

Moreover, once account is taken of the marginal difference in distance between transferring on to Watling Street or staying on the North Downs trackways to Canterbury, then in terms of the 'Paddlesworth choice', maintaining the well-defined route along the escarpment may have appeared more attractive than many commentators have previously thought. In addition, the ease of route-finding without maps by following the scarp, with its well-defined features, was undoubtedly an important factor for the medieval traveller. Concerns regarding crime and safety, as well as the relative seclusion of the trackway away from but within easy reach of the spring-line villages, may also have served as a positive rather than a negative factor for medieval pilgrims. Blink and the villein working in the field would miss the daily pilgrims as they passed by on the distant hillside.

9

Conclusion

The thirteenth-century merchant capitalist and pilgrim, Richard of Southwick, in many respects personifies the Pilgrims' Way story. For like most of Chaucer's pilgrims, Richard was a relatively successful man of his time. Furthermore, he had escaped the rigidities and confines of rural feudalism. This was apparent from his cosmopolitan lifestyle and reflected in his taste for wines from southern France, fashionable footwear in a variety of styles and a taste for food from across the Continent. Richard was very much a part of the life of the port town of Southampton and seized the opportunities it held. He was a modern man who operated within the freedoms that the town offered and had made his own way as a successful merchant. Yet despite being at the forefront of world trade and commerce, Richard of Southwick also had roots set in a world of belief, ritual and miracles. Most importantly for the Pilgrims' Way story, his lifestyle still included the veneration of saints.

As to the route Richard of Southwick took to Canterbury – it remains a mystery. Nevertheless, from the evidence of early maps, our knowledge of the medieval road system and the itineraries of medieval kings, it is not unreasonable to suggest that a route incorporating the trackways along the edge of the North Downs escarpment was one of a number of possibilities. Certainly, if Southwick chose to make his pilgrimage by road, evidence suggests that because of a lack of roads running from west to east, combined with extremely poor going underfoot, his route may well have remained north of the Kent and Sussex Weald. Yet we can only guess whether or not he chose to follow the trackways traversing the edge of the downs or kept to the trackways that linked the towns and villages in the Vale of Holmesdale. This is exactly the dilemma we have when drawing on the evidence of the royal itineraries. Within Southwick's own lifetime we know that Edward I travelled between Guildford

47 Hyde Abbey Gate, Winchester, Pilgrims' Way

and Canterbury, calling at towns close to or on the route of the Pilgrims' Way, but as to the exact route he took, this again is a matter for conjecture.

In terms of the evidence, it is not unreasonable to conclude that the roads and trackways that much later were to become known as the Pilgrims' Way offered a viable route for Southwick, should he have chosen to use them. The clarity of the route in terms of its distinct geographical features, certainly for the significant sections along the edge of the North Downs, is self-evident. Moreover, the benefits that the route held in respect of superior drainage and firm going underfoot have been well established.

We have also seen how a number of commentators implied that alternative routes were of less distance than the Pilgrims' Way and suggested medieval travellers either took the route shown on the Gough map from Guildford through London via Ripley and Kingston or, when reaching Paddlesworth, chose to transfer on to Watling Street at Rochester. Such alternatives have been referred to as more direct, straight, less laborious or even more convenient. However, we have seen that the distance between Guildford and Canterbury via London or the alternative of transferring on to Watling Street at Rochester was so marginal as not to make any appreciable difference.

It has also been argued that crime may well have been a significant factor that deterred medieval travellers from using certain routes and evidence suggests that certain stretches along Watling Street had acquired a particularly infamous reputation. It was also noted that there were other risks associated with medieval travel, particularly for a stranger travelling away from their own manor. As such, the course taken by the Pilgrims' Way, which for the most part maintains a discreet distance from the spring-line villages, may well have been considered a benefit by many medieval travellers.

Critics of the Pilgrims' Way have argued that villages and towns along the route did not have the infrastructure to cater for the numbers of travellers that would have used the way. Their contention is that the trackway was insufficient to carry the hordes of pilgrims making their way to Canterbury. However, examination of the level of offerings made at Becket's shrine, together with consideration of people's position within the feudal social hierarchy, suggests that the actual numbers who would have been able to leave the manor and undertake an extended pilgrimage was far less than has been commonly accepted. By far the greatest proportion of people worked on the land. Far fewer people in a feudal society would have been in a position to leave the land for any length of time – even if they had so desired. When it came to numbers of pilgrims, the enthusiasm of the Victorian and Edwardian pilgrimists undoubtedly over-egged the pudding. As such, there is little reason to conclude that the infrastructure of the spring-line villages was insufficient to sustain the limited number of pilgrims.

Much of the theory expressed by the pilgrimists left itself open to criticism. Perhaps both Belloc and Cartwright, who did so much to popularise the Pilgrims' Way, presented their readers with a trail based upon as many tenuous assertions as credible evidence. Similarly, Captain E.R. James' own evidence for the numerous inclusions of the Pilgrims' Road on the first edition Ordnance Survey maps also suffered in terms of credibility, placing great emphasis on the dates of fairs being fixed to coincide with the passage of pilgrims to and from Canterbury. Neither did Captain James' identification of scenes from Bunyan's allegorical pilgrimage with locations found along a route of worldly pilgrimage help sustain his case. It was Wilfrid Hooper who wrote 'probably the Way owes more to Bunyan than he ever owed to the Way'.[1]

The work of Edwin Hart, Ivan Margary and many others, who have leant much credibility to the view of the Way as a route predating medieval pilgrimage should not be overlooked. Margary was bold enough to assert that the trackway is one of the most important in Britain and argued that it was 'the main route by which early Man could penetrate readily into this island from the Continent, and indeed he probably began using it before the separation of the island occurred'. For this alone the Pilgrims' Way rightly merits the opening lines that Belloc bestowed on it: 'Of all these primal things the least obvious but the most important is The Road.'[2]

The story of the Pilgrims' Way, like all history, is not static. It is because people continued to walk it, lobby for its incorporation as a long-distance footpath, search for it, write about it and, essentially, believe in it that is still resonates with us today. Perhaps most importantly, it is still used as a route of pilgrimage to Canterbury and by numbers of people that may well exceed their medieval predecessors.

The narrative of the Pilgrims' Way will continue to develop, adapt and change. It is a story that will respond to new archaeological finds, such as the sections of the way discovered close to the White Horse Stone during work on the Channel Tunnel Rail Link excavations. The Pilgrims' Way story will continue because essentially it is a story for all of us, who once, at the beginning of a day, surveyed the chalk escarpment that lay ahead to see where the journey would lead us, before casting an eye back along the chalk to the place from whence we had come. For those are the very days when we could believe Julia Cartwright when she wrote: 'By many a Kentish homestead the grassy track still winds its way along the lonely hill-side overlooking the blue Weald, and if you ask its name, the labourer who guides the plough, or the waggoner driving his team, will tell that it is the Pilgrims' Road to Canterbury.'[3]

Appendix

Flowcharts of the Belloc and Cartwright Routes

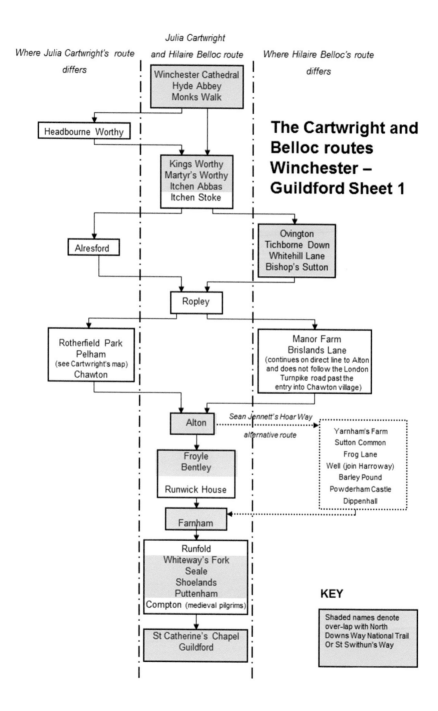

Where Julia Cartwright's route
differs

*Julia Cartwright
and Hilaire Belloc route*

Where Hilaire Belloc's route
differs

Winchester Cathedral
Hyde Abbey
Monks Walk

**The Cartwright and
Belloc routes
Winchester –
Guildford Sheet 1**

Headbourne Worthy

Kings Worthy
Martyr's Worthy
Itchen Abbas
Itchen Stoke

Alresford

Ovington
Tichborne Down
Whitehill Lane
Bishop's Sutton

Ropley

Rotherfield Park
Pelham
(see Cartwright's map)
Chawton

Manor Farm
Brislands Lane
(continues on direct line to Alton
and does not follow the London
Turnpike road past the
entry into Chawton village)

Alton

*Sean Jennett's Hoar Way
alternative route*

Yarnham's Farm
Sutton Common
Frog Lane
Well (join Harroway)
Barley Pound
Powderham Castle
Dippenhall

Froyle
Bentley

Runwick House

Farnham

Runfold
Whiteway's Fork
Seale
Shoelands
Puttenham
Compton (medieval pilgrims)

KEY

St Catherine's Chapel
Guildford

Shaded names denote
over-lap with North
Downs Way National Trail
Or St Swithun's Way

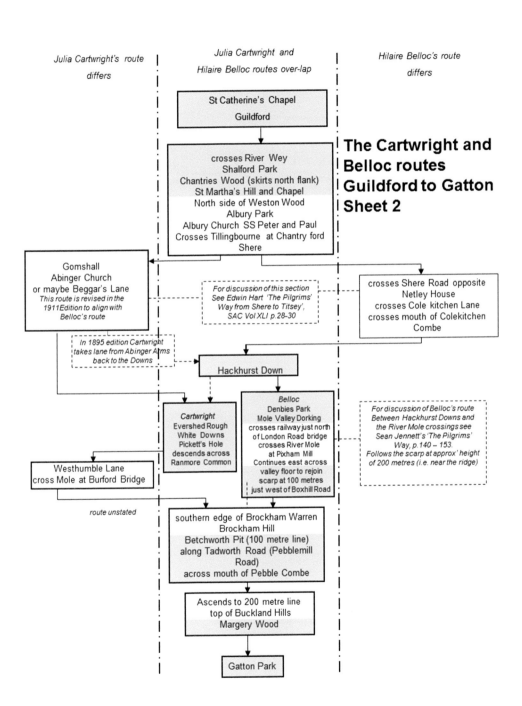

Julia Cartwright's route differs

Julia Cartwright and Hilaire Belloc routes over-lap

Hilaire Belloc's route differs

St Catherine's Chapel
Guildford

crosses River Wey
Shalford Park
Chantries Wood (skirts north flank)
St Martha's Hill and Chapel
North side of Weston Wood
Albury Park
Albury Church SS Peter and Paul
Crosses Tillingbourne at Chantry ford
Shere

The Cartwright and Belloc routes Guildford to Gatton Sheet 2

Gomshall
Abinger Church
or maybe Beggar's Lane
This route is revised in the 1911 Edition to align with Belloc's route

For discussion of this section
See Edwin Hart 'The Pilgrims'
Way from Shere to Titsey',
SAC Vol XLI p.28-30

crosses Shere Road opposite
Netley House
crosses Cole kitchen Lane
crosses mouth of Colekitchen
Combe

In 1895 edition Cartwright
takes lane from Abinger Arms
back to the Downs

Hackhurst Down

Cartwright
Eversshed Rough
White Downs
Pickett's Hole
descends across
Ranmore Common

Belloc
Denbies Park
Mole Valley Dorking
crosses railway just north
of London Road bridge
crosses River Mole
at Pixham Mill
Continues east across
valley floor to rejoin
scarp at 100 metres
just west of Boxhill Road

For discussion of Belloc's route
Between Hackhurst Downs and
the River Mole crossings see
Sean Jennett's 'The Pilgrims'
Way, p.140 – 153.
Follows the scarp at approx' height
of 200 metres (i.e. near the ridge)

Westhumble Lane
cross Mole at Burford Bridge

route unstated

southern edge of Brockham Warren
Brockham Hill
Betchworth Pit (100 metre line)
along Tadworth Road (Pebblemill
Road)
across mouth of Pebble Combe

Ascends to 200 metre line
top of Buckland Hills
Margery Wood

Gatton Park

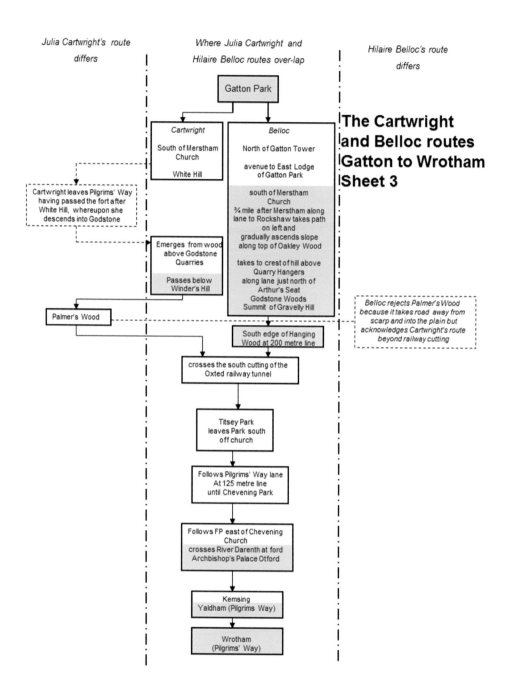

Julia Cartwright's route differs

Where Julia Cartwright and Hilaire Belloc routes over-lap

Hilaire Belloc's route differs

The Cartwright and Belloc routes Gatton to Wrotham Sheet 3

Gatton Park

Cartwright — South of Merstham Church — White Hill

Belloc — North of Gatton Tower — avenue to East Lodge of Gatton Park — south of Merstham Church ¾ mile after Merstham along lane to Rockshaw takes path on left and gradually ascends slope along top of Oakley Wood — takes to crest of hill above Quarry Hangers along lane just north of Arthur's Seat Godstone Woods Summit of Gravelly Hill

Cartwright leaves Pilgrims' Way having passed the fort after White Hill, whereupon she descends into Godstone

Emerges from wood above Godstone Quarries — Passes below Winder's Hill

Palmer's Wood

Belloc rejects Palmer's Wood because it takes road away from scarp and into the plain but acknowledges Cartwright's route beyond railway cutting

South edge of Hanging Wood at 200 metre line

crosses the south cutting of the Oxted railway tunnel

Titsey Park leaves Park south off church

Follows Pilgrims' Way lane At 125 metre line until Chevening Park

Follows FP east of Chevening Church crosses River Darenth at ford Archbishop's Palace Otford

Kemsing Yaldham (Pilgrims Way)

Wrotham (Pilgrims' Way)

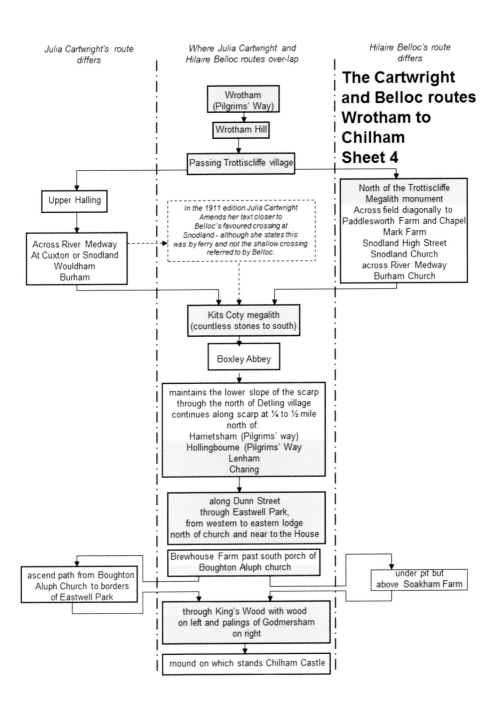

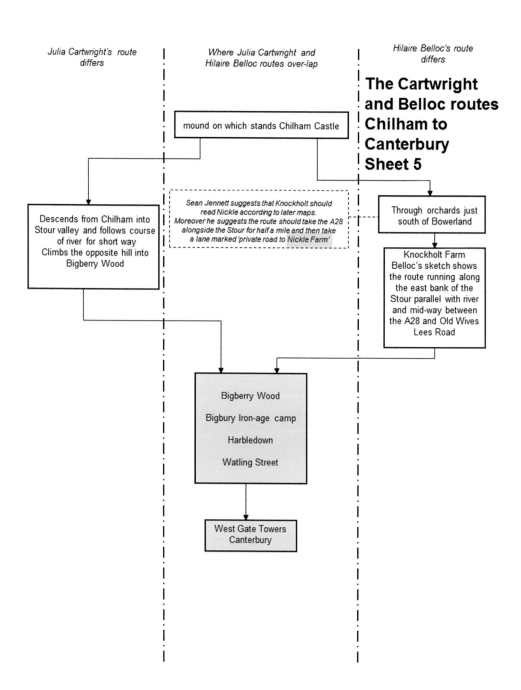

Julia Cartwright's route differs

Where Julia Cartwright and Hilaire Belloc routes over-lap

Hilaire Belloc's route differs

The Cartwright and Belloc routes Chilham to Canterbury Sheet 5

mound on which stands Chilham Castle

Descends from Chilham into Stour valley and follows course of river for short way Climbs the opposite hill into Bigberry Wood

Sean Jennett suggests that Knockholt should read Nickle according to later maps. Moreover he suggests the route should take the A28 alongside the Stour for half a mile and then take a lane marked 'private road to Nickle Farm'

Through orchards just south of Bowerland

Knockholt Farm Belloc's sketch shows the route running along the east bank of the Stour parallel with river and mid-way between the A28 and Old Wives Lees Road

Bigberry Wood

Bigbury Iron-age camp

Harbledown

Watling Street

West Gate Towers Canterbury

Notes

Introduction A Hidden Byway Through Time

1 Elliston-Erwood, F.C., 'The Pilgrims' Way, its antiquity and its alleged medieval use', *Archaeologia Cantiana Volume 37* (1925), p. 1.
2 Ure, John, *Pilgrimages, the great adventure of the middle ages* (Carroll & Graf, 2006), pp. 110–3.
3 Belloc, Hilaire, *The Old Road* (Constable & Co., 1921), p. 4.
4 Margary, Ivan D., 'The North Downs Main Trackway and the Pilgrims' Way', *Archaeological Journal Volume 119*, p. 39.
5 Rackham Oliver, *Illustrated History of the English Countryside* (Phoenix, 1997), p. 14.

1 The Pilgrims' Way in the Landscape

1 Brandon, Peter, *The North Downs* (Phillimore & Co., 2005), p. 14.
2 Wenban-Smith, Francis, 'The Palaeolithic Archaeology of Kent', ed. John H. Williams, *The Archaeology of Kent to AD 800* (Boydell Press), p. 31.
3 Mesolithic, middle Stone Age, 10,000–6000 BC and Neolithic, late Stone Age, 7000–2500 BC.
4 Champion, Timothy, *The Archaeology of Kent to AD 800*, ed. John H. Williams (The Boydell Press, 2007), Chapter 2, p. 72.
5 Scott, Beccy, 'Kentish Evidence of the Palaeolithic and Mesolithic Periods', *An Historical Atlas of Kent*, ed. T. Lawson & D. Killingray (Phillimore, 2004), p. 7.
6 Champion, *op. cit.*, p. 84.
7 *Ibid.*, pp. 96–7.
8 Owen, Elizabeth & Frost, Mark, *The Dover Bronze Age Boat Guide* (The Dover Bronze Age Boat Trust), p. 17.
9 Champion, *op. cit.,* p. 114.
10 Yates, Dave, 'Kent in the Bronze Age: Land, Power and prestige *c.* 1500–700 BC', ed. T. Lawson & D. Killingray, *An Historical Atlas of Kent* (Phillimore, 2004), p. 13.
11 Tuson, Dan, *The Kent Downs* (Tempus, 2007), p. 16.
12 Brandon, Peter, *The North Downs* (Phillimore & Co., 2005), p. 2.

13 Flight, Colin, *Early printed maps of Kent*. Digital archive of material deposited by researchers, Kent Archaeological Society, http://www.kentarchaeology.ac/digiarchive/digiarch.html. Flight notes that it has been suggested that Speed's map is also a rather poor copy of the original Symonson map.

14 Cobbett, William, *Rural Rides*, Everyman's Library (J.M. Dent & Sons Ltd, 1932), p. 252.

15 Ashbee, Paul, *Kent in Prehistoric Times* (Tempus, 2005), p. 101.

16 *Ibid*, p. 101.

17 Wenban-Smith, Francis, 'The Palaeolithic Archaeology of Kent', ed. John H. Williams, *The Archaeology of Kent to AD 800*, (Boydell Press), p. 80.

18 Margary, Ivan D., 'The North Downs Main Trackway and the Pilgrims' Way', *Archaeological Journal Volume 119*, p. 42.

19 *Ibid.*, p.40.

20 Belloc, Hilaire, *The Old Road* (Constable & Co., 1911), p. 25.

21 Timperley, H.W. & Brill, Edith, *Ancient Trackways of Wessex* (Nonsuch, 1965, this edition 2005), p. 82.

22 Hanworth & Hastings, F.A., *Surrey Archaeology Collections Volume 58* (1961–63), p. 10, quoting Crawford, O.G.S., 'Archaeology in the Field' (1953), pp. 78–9.

23 Timperley H.W. and Brill, Edith, *op. cit.*, p. 18.

24 Belsey, Valerie, *The Green Lanes of England* (Green Books, 1998), p. 32.

25 Belloc, Hilaire, *The Old Road*, (Constable & Co., 1921), p. 16.

26 Taylor, *Roads and Tracks of Britain* (Orion, 1994), p. 19.

27 Ravilious, Kate, *National Geographic News*, 13 October 2010.

28 Champion, Tim, 'Prehistoric Kent', ed. John H. Williams, *The Archaeology of Kent to AD 800* (Boydell Press, 2007), p. 80.

29 *Ibid.*, p. 20.

30 Killick, Sean, 'Neolithic Landscape and Experience: The Medway Megaliths', under 'Archaeological Note and Summaries', in *Archaeologica Cantiana Volume 130* (2010), p. 348.

31 Cochrane, C., *The Lost Roads of Wessex* (Pan Books Ltd, 1972), p. 12.

32 Hippisley-Cox, R., *The Green Roads of England* (first published 1914, this edition, Methuen & Co., 1948), p. 98.

33 Massingham, H.J., *English Downland* (B.T. Batsford Ltd, 1942/3), p. 103.

34 Allen, Grant, *Science in Arcady* (Lawrence & Bullen, 1892), pp. 229–30.

35 *Ibid.*, pp. 212–30.

36 *Ibid.*

37 Cartwright, Julia, *The Pilgrims' Way – from Winchester to Canterbury* (J.S. Virtue & Co., Ltd, 1895); Julia Cartwright was also a novelist writing under the name of Mrs Henry Ady.

38 *Ibid.*, p. 5.

39 Elliston-Erwood, F.C., *Archaeologia Cantiana Volume 37* (1925), p. 8.

40 Champion, Timothy, 'Prehistoric Kent', *The Archaeology of Kent to AD 800* (Boydell Press, 2007), p. 95.

41 *Ibid.*

42 Jessop, Frank W., *Kent History Illustrated* (Kent County Council, 1966), p. 15.

43 Taylor, Christopher, *Roads and Tracks of Britain* (Orion, 1994), p. 7.

44 Belloc, Hilaire, *The Old Road* (London: Constable, 1921), p. 43.

45 *Ibid.*, p. 45.

46 *Ibid.*, p. 28.

47 *Ibid.*, p. 56.

48 Margary, Ivan D., 'The North Downs Main Trackway and the Pilgrims' Way', *Archaeological Journal Volume 109*, p. 39.

49 Stanley, Arthur P., *Historical Memorials of Canterbury* (1912), includes essays by Dean Stanley in 1854–55 and, most importantly, Albert Way's essay in Note D of Appendix, entitled 'The Pilgrims Way or Path towards the Shrine of St Thomas of Canterbury' (1855), p. 165.

2 Towards a Pilgrims' Way Theory

1 Taylor, Christopher, *Roads and Tracks of Britain* (Orion, 1994), p. 10.

2 Margary, *op. cit.*, p. 53.

3 *Ibid.*

4 *Ibid.*

5 Belloc, *op. cit.*, pp. 69–70.

6 Kent County Council, *Historic Buildings, Sites and Monuments Record*, 30 January 2004; SMR Number TR 15 NW 33–KE4844.

7 Ashbee, Paul, *Kent in Prehistoric Times* (Tempus, 2005), p. 160.

8 Sparey-Green, Christopher, Canterbury Archaeological Trust, *Kent Archaeological Society Newsletter* Issue No 86, Winter 2010, pp. 14–5.

9 Cartwright, Julia, *The Pilgrims' Way – from Winchester to Canterbury* (J.S. Virtue & Co., Ltd, 1893), p. 131.

10 Cartwright, Julia, *The Pilgrims' Way – from Winchester to Canterbury* (John Murray, 1911), p. vi.

11 *Ibid.*, pp. 185–6.

12 Cartwright Julia, *The Pilgrims Way – from Winchester to Canterbury* (Wildwood House, 1982).

13 Jennet, Sean, *The Pilgrims' Way* (Cassell, 1971), p. 63.

14 *Ibid.*

15 Crump, E.R., *History* (June 1936), p. 25.

16 *Ibid.*, p.26: Crump's summation of Way's argument in which he also states that 'after Charing Mr Way becomes a little doubtful of the exact course of the road. It has of course to be taken to Canterbury'.

17 Oledzka, E., 'The Creating of the National and Regional Prehistoric, Medieval and Post-Medieval Archaeological Collections in the Light of A. Way's Correspondence with A.W. Franks: a Survey of A.Way's Letters Held by The British Museum, Department of Prehistory and Europe' (London: British Museum Research Publications, British Museum Press, forthcoming).

18 Way, Albert, 'The Pilgrims' Way or path towards the shrine of St. Thomas of Canterbury', Appendix D to Arthur P. Stanley's *Historical Memorials of Canterbury* (London: John Murray, 1912), p. 264.

19 Margary, Ivan D., 'The North Downs Main Trackway and the Pilgrims' Way', *Archaeological Journal Volume 109*, p. 40; and Hart, E., 'The Prehistoric Road called the Pilgrims' Way in East Surrey' [manuscript], Edwin Hart Collection, 347/6, Guildford: Surrey Archaeological Society.

20 Hart, Edwin FSA, 'The Pilgrims' Way from Shere to Titsey as traced by public records and remains', *Surrey Archaeological Collections Volume 41*, 1933, p. 1.

21 Hart, Edwin, 'The Prehistoric Road called the Pilgrims' Way in East Surrey' [manuscript], Edwin Hart Collection, 347/6, Guildford: Surrey Archaeology Society, p. 4.

22 Brandon, Peter, *The Kent and Sussex Weald* (Phillimore & Co., 2003), p. 177.

23 *Ibid.*

24 Ohler, Norbert, *The Medieval Traveller* (Boydell Press, 1989), p. 26.

25 Margary, *op. cit.*, p. 42.

3 Cartographers and the Pilgrims' Way

1 Hart, Edwin FSA, 'The Pilgrims' Way from Shere to Titsey', *Surrey Archaeological Collections Volume 41*, 1933, p. 2.

2 *Ibid.*, p. 5; Hart is referring to Rocque's map of Surrey, 1764–70.

3 *Ibid.*, p. 3.

4 Gilchrist, R. & Reynolds, A. (eds), *Reflections: 50 Years of Medieval Archaeology, 1957–2007* (Leeds, 2009), p. 423.

5 Reynolds, A., 'Anglo-Saxon and medieval period: burial, settlement and the structure of landscape', in H. Glass et al., *Tracks Through Time, The Archaeology of the Channel Tunnel Rail Link* (Oxford, OA).

6 Elliston-Erwood, F.C., *The Pilgrims' Road* (The Homeland Association, 1923), p. 36.

7 Gairdner, James (ed.), 'The Paston letters AD 1422–1509', New Complete Library Edition, Volume 5 (Constable, 1904), p. 112.

8 Jennett, Sean, *The Pilgrims' Way – from Winchester to Canterbury* (Cassell & Co., 1971), p. 15.

9 Ravensdale, Jack, *In the Steps of Chaucer's Pilgrims* (Guild Publishing, 1989), pp. 15–21.

10 *Ibid.*, p. 63.

11 Ravensdale, Jack, *In the Steps of Chaucer's Pilgrims* (Guild Publishing, 1989), p. 20.

12 Note: only the Aylesford Bridge (road) crossing exists today. There is no longer a ferry-crossing at either Snodland or Halling. The Snodland ferry closed in 1948: Ashbee, Andrew, *Around Snodland* (The History Press), p. 12.

13 Hooper, Wilfrid, *Surrey Archaeological Collections Volume 44* (1936), p. 55.

14 Elliston-Erwood, F.C., 'Miscellaneous notes on some Kent roads', *Archaeologia Cantiana Volume 70* (1956), p. 203.

15 Elliston-Erwood, F.C., 'The Pilgrims' Way, its antiquity and its alleged medieval use', *Archaeologia Cantiana Volume 37* (1925), pp. 3–4.

16 Furley, Robert, FSA, *A History of the Weald of Kent Volume II* (Ashford: Henry Igglesden; London: John Russell Smith, 1874), p. 641.

17 *Ibid.*, pp. 631–47.

18 *Ibid.*, p. 641.

19 Furley, Robert, FSA, *A History of the Weald of Kent Volume I* (Ashford: Henry Igglesden; London: John Russell Smith, 1871), p. 415.

20 Curtis, Neil & Walker, Jim, *North Downs Way National Trail Guide* (Aurum Press, 2005), p. 20.

21 James, Captain E. Renouard, *Notes on the Pilgrims' Way in West Surrey* (London: Edward Stanford, 1871), p. 5.

22 *Ibid.*, p. 16.

23 Elliston-Erwood, F.C., *The Pilgrims' Way, its antiquity and its alleged mediaeval use*; *ibid.*, Volume 37, p. 55.

24 *Ibid.*

25 James, Captain E. Renouard, *Notes on the Pilgrims Way in West Surrey* (London: Edward Stanford, 1871), p. 22.

26 Ure, John, *Pilgrimages – The Great Adventure of the Middle Ages* (Carroll & Graff, 2006), pp. 213–14. For fuller discussion on writers and post-Reformation views of pilgrimage see John Ure, *op. cit.*, Chapter 16 'John Bunyan, the Allegorical Pilgrim', pp. 209–21.

27 Manning & Bray, *The History and Antiquities of the County of Surrey Volume II* (1804–14), p. 253; this quote is taken from C.G. Crump's 'The Pilgrims' Way', *History Quarterly* (June 1936).

28 *Ibid.*, p. 408.

4 From Pilgrims' Way to North Downs Way

1 *All Saints Church Boughton Aluph, A Short History* (Kent: Crown Print & Design), p. 5.

2 Hooper, Wilfrid, 'The Pilgrims' Way and its supposed pilgrims use', *Surrey Archaeological Collections Volume 44* (1936), p. 64.

3 Cartwright, *op. cit.* (1982), p. 10.

4 Ward, Snowden H., *The Canterbury Pilgrimages* (Adam & Charles Black, 1904), p. 308.

5 Belloc, *op. cit.*, p. 103.

6 Cartwright, *op. cit.*, p. 6.

7 Jennett, Sean, *The Pilgrims' Way from Winchester to Canterbury* (Cassell, 1971), p. 9.

8 Rackham, Oliver, *The Illustrated History of the Countryside* (Phoenix, 1997), p. 15.

9 Taylor, Christopher, *Roads and Tracks of Britain* (Orion, 1994), p. 154.

10 *Ibid.*, p. 161.

11 Way, Albert, Appendix D to Stanley, Arthur P., *Historical Memorials of Canterbury* (John Murray, 1855), p. 221.

12 *Special Committee on Footpaths and Access to the Countryside* (Cmd. 7207, September 1947), the Hobhouse Committee.

13 National Parks and Access to the Countryside Act, 1949.

14 Herbstein, Denis, *The North Downs Way* (HMSO, 1982), p. 3.

15 Ministry of Town and County Planning Archives, National Archives, HLC/92/39.

16 The Countryside Commission was established in 1968 and took over the work of the National 45 Parks Commission established in 1949. The author has used both terms as interchangeable.

17 Long Distance Route Committee Agenda 23/7/63 Minute 428: Proposed PW/NDW Kent and Hants Path, COU1/1376 National Archives.

5 The Belloc and Cartwright Routes

1 Knocker, Captain H.W., 'The Valley of Holmesdale – its evolution and development', *Archaeologia Cantiana Volume 31* (1915), p. 158.

2 *Ibid.*, pp. 156–7.
3 *Ibid.*, p. 159.
4 *Ibid.*

6 Medieval Travellers on the Pilgrims' Way

1 Crump, C.G., 'The Pilgrims' Way', *History Quarterly* (June 1936), p. 33.
2 *Ibid.*, p. 33.
3 Hindle, Brian Paul, PhD, FRGS, *Medieval Roads* (Shire Publications Ltd, 2nd edn, 1989), pp. 13–5.
4 Taylor, Christopher, *Roads and Tracks of Britain* (Orion, 1994), p. xi.
5 Cochrane, C., *The Lost Roads of Wessex* (Pan Books, 1972), p. 52.
6 'Roman Roads East of Winchester – The Search for a Winchester to London Road', in the Hampshire Filed Club Newsletter, http://surreyarchaeology.org.uk/node/167.
7 Gough, Henry, *Itinerary of King Edward the First throughout His Reign, Volume II 1286–1307* (Paisley Alexander Gardener, 1900).
8 Hindle, Paul, *Medieval Roads* (Shire Archaeology, 2nd edn, 1989), p. 14.
9 Gough, Henry, *op. cit.*, p. 60
10 Taylor, Christopher, *Roads and Tracks of Britain* (Orion, 1994), p. 114.
11 Gough, Henry, *op. cit.*, pp. 121, 186.
12 Crump, *op. cit.*, p. 33.
13 Lawson, Terence, 'Historical Research Notes', *Archaeologia Cantiana Volume 130* (Kent Archaeological Society, 2010), p. 388.
14 *Ibid.*, p. 389.
15 Gough, Henry, *op. cit.*, p. 213.
16 *Ibid.*, p. 121.
17 Cochrane, C., *The Lost Roads of Wessex* (Pan Books, 1972), p. 56.
18 Weston, David, 'Roman Roads East of Winchester – 1', *Hampshire Field Club and Archaeological Society Newsletter 49* (spring 2008), p. 21.
19 Hooper, Wilfred, ILD, 'The Pilgrims' Way and its supposed pilgrim use', *Surrey Archaeological Collections Volume 44* (1936), p. 79.
20 Way, Albert, 'The Pilgrims Way or Path towards the Shrine of St Thomas of Canterbury', in Arthur P. Stanley, *Historical Memorials of Canterbury* (Murray, 1912), p. 260.
21 Hooper, Wilfred, ILD, *op. cit.*, pp. 53–4.
22 Ohler, Norbert, *The Medieval Traveller* (Boydell Press, 1989), p. 26.
23 Jennett, Sean, *The Pilgrims' Way from Winchester to Canterbury* (Cassell, 1971), p. 183.
24 Belloc, *op. cit.*, Hyde, 1921, p. 223.
25 Webb, Diana, *Pilgrimage in Medieval England* (Hambledon & London, 2000), pp. 234–5.
26 *Ibid.*, p. 237.
27 Ward, Snowden H. , *The Canterbury Pilgrimages* (Adam & Charles Black, 1904), pp. 90–1.
28 Stanley, Arthur P., *Historical Memorials of Canterbury* (Murray, 1912), p.98.
   ★ Fitztstephen's account; ★★ Garnier's account.
29 Platt, Colin, 'The Merchant Capitalists Part III 1300–1400', *Medieval Southampton – the post and trading community* (Routledge & Kegan Paul, 1973), pp. 103–4.

30 Webb, Diana, *Pilgrimage in Medieval England* (Hambledon & London, 2000), p. 212.

31 Platt, *op. cit.*, p. 28.

32 Lawson, Terence, 'Historical Research Notes', the details of Kent shown on the mid-fourteenth century Gough map, *Archaeologia Cantiana Volume 130* (2010), p. 389.

33 See, Calow, David, 'Investigation of a possible Roman road between Bighton and Medstead', *Hampshire Field Club & Archaeological Society Newsletter 53* (autumn 2010), p. 8; and Weston, David, 'Roman Roads East of Winchester – 1', *Hampshire Filed Club and Archaeological Society Newsletter 49* (spring 2008), p. 21.

7 The Paddlesworth Choice

1 Thornhill, Patrick, 'The Medway Crossings of the Pilgrims Way', *Archaeologia Cantiana Volume 89* (1974).

2 Belsey, Valerie, *The Green Lanes of England* (Green Books Ltd, 1998), p. 30. Belsey suggests that the Pilgrims' Way and the Icknield Way date back to the time when man the hunter first followed the tracks of wild animals.

3 Brandon, Peter, *The Kent and Sussex Weald* (Phillimore, 2003), p. 43.

4 *Ibid.*, p. 44.

5 Lower, Mark Anthony, *History of Sussex Volume 1* (London: John Russell Mith, 1870), p. 22.

6 Bannister, Dr Nicola, *The Cultural Heritage of woodlands in the South East*, South East AONBs Woodlands Programme, October 2007, p. 7.

7 Belloc, Hilaire, *The Old Road* (Constable & Co., 1921) (Belloc discusses the crossing of the Medway in the Wrotham to Boxley section, pp. 231–55).

8 British Library Manuscript Add: 42715. Volume 1. Surveys, made 1557–60 (with later additions at the ends of some of the sections) in connection with the disgavelling of the estates of Sir Edward Wotton (to whom Thomas Wotton had succeeded at the time of the survey) in consequence of a private Act of Parliament.

9 Fielding, Rev. C.H., *Memories of Malling and its Valley* (West Malling, 1893). Information regarding the *Wotton Survey* and *Memories of Malling* kindly provided by Dr Andrew Ashbee at the Snodland Museum.

10 Cartwright, Julia, *The Pilgrims' Way – from Winchester to Canterbury* (John Murray, 1911), p. 137.

11 Margary, Ivan D., 'The North Downs Main Trackway and the Pilgrims' Way', *Archaeological Journal Volume 109*, p. 40.

12 *Ibid.*

13 Hawkes, Professor, *Hants Field Club*, Proc., Volume 9, p. 324, referred to by Margary in *Surrey Archaeological Collections Volume 52*, 1950–51, 'The North Downs Main Trackways', pp. 29–30.

14 Jusserand, J.J., *English Wayfaring Life in the Middle Ages* (T. Fisher Unwin, 1909), p. 151.

15 Stanley, Arthur P., *Historical Memorials of Canterbury* (1912); includes essays written by Dean Stanley in 1854–55, pp. 210–1.

16 Mortimer, Ian, *The Time Traveller's Guide to Medieval England* (Vintage Books, 2009), p. 125.

17 Hindle, Brian Paul, *Medieval Roads* (Shire Archaeology, 1989), pp. 6–7.

18 Jusserand, *op. cit.*, p. 36.

19 Brayley, Edward, *Topographical History of Surrey*, quoted by C.G. Crump in *History Quarterly* (June 1936), p. 24.

20 Crump, C.G., *History Quarterly* (June 1936), p. 25.

21 *Ibid.*

22 Goodsall, Robert H., *The Ancient Road to Canterbury – A Progress through Kent* (1960), p. 3.

23 *Ibid.*, p. 4.

24 *Ibid.*

25 Webb, Diana, *Pilgrimage in Medieval England* (Hambledon & London, 2000), p. 221.

26 Ravensdale, Jack, *In the Steps of Chaucer's Pilgrims* (Guild Publishing, 1989), p. 19.

27 Mortimer, Ian, *The Time Traveller's Guide to Medieval England* (Vintage, 2009), p. 223. Mortimer's summation of Summerson's findings in *Structure of Law Enforcement*, p. 326.

28 Jusserand, J.J., *English Wayfaring Life in the Middle Ages* (T. Fisher Unwin, 1909), p. 261.

29 Webb, Diana, *Pilgrimage in Medieval England* (Hambledown & London, 2000), p. 231.

30 Jusserand, *op. cit.*, pp. 256–8.

31 Lawson & Killingray (eds), *An Historical Atlas of Kent* (Phillimore, 2004), Chapter 14, Guy Banyard, p. 34.

32 Cartwright, Julia, *The Pilgrims' Way – from Winchester to Canterbury* (John Murray, 1911), p. 141.

33 James, Captain E.R., *Notes on the Pilgrims' Way in West Surrey* (London: Edward Stanford, 1871), p. 21.

34 Elliston–Erwood, F.C., *The Pilgrims' Road* (The Homeland Association, 1923), p. 31.

35 *Ibid.*, p. 9.

36 Finch, William Coles, *In Kentish Pilgrims Land* (C.W. Daniel Co., 1925), pp. 81–2.

37 Stanley, Arthur P., *Historical Memorials of Canterbury* (1912), includes essays written by Dean Stanley in 1854 and 1855 and Albert Way's essay in Note D of Appendix entitled 'The Pilgrims' Way or Path towards the Shrine of St Thomas of Canterbury', 1855.

38 Webb, Diana, *Pilgrimage in Medieval England* (Hambledown & London, 2000), p. 222.

39 Way, Albert, 'The Pilgrims' Way or Path towards the Shrine of St Thomas of Canterbury', Appendix D in Arthur P. Stanley, *op. cit.* (John Murray, 1912), p. 260.

40 *Ibid.*, p. 248.

41 Rackham, Oliver, *The Illustrated History of the Countryside* (Phoenix Illustrated, 1997), p. 36.

42 Champion, Timothy, *The Archaeology of Kent to AD 800*, John H. Williams (ed.) (Boydell Press, 2007), p. 74.

43 Thornhill, Patrick, 'The Medway Crossings of the Pilgrims' Way', *Archaeologia Cantiana Volume 89* (1974), p. 94.

44 Champion, Timothy, *The Archaeology of Kent to AD 800*, John H. Williams (ed.) (Boydell Press, 2007), p. 73.

45 *Ibid.*, p. 72.

46 Ashbee, Paul, *Kent in Prehistoric Times* (Tempus, 2005), p. 98.

47 *Ibid.*, pp. 87–118.

48 Champion, *op. cit.*, p. 124; Ashbee, *ibid.*, p. 125.

49 Ashbee, *ibid.*, p. 150; the quotation from Ashbee also contains within it a quotation from Pretty (1862).

50 *Ibid.*, p. 149.

51 Champion, *op. cit.*, p. 95.

52 Cartwright, *op. cit.*, pp. 4–5; Belloc, *op. cit.*, pp. 21, 88; Belloc merely touches on the metals of the Devonian peninsula and the growth of the Sussex Weald iron industry, but does not refer to Grant Allen, unlike Cartwright. Grant Allen's tin road theory, published in *Cornhill Magazine*, November 1889, 'The Bronze Axe', originally taken as abstract from Allen Grant, *Science in Arcady* (London: Lawrence & Bullen), Chapter 12, p. 212 and Chapter 13, p. 231.

53 Watt Francis, *Canterbury Pilgrims and their Ways* (Methuen & Co. Ltd, 1917), p. 222.

54 Finch, William Coles, *In Kentish Pilgrims Land* (C.W. Daniel Co., 1925), p. 295.

55 Fergusson, James, DCL, FRS, *Rude Stone Monuments, their Ages and Uses* (John Murray, 1872), p. 117.

56 Wright, Christopher John, *A Guide to the Pilgrims' Way and North Downs Way* (1993), p. 200.

57 Ashbee, *op. cit.*, p. 115.

58 Goodsall, Robert H., *The Ancient Road to Canterbury – A Progress through Kent* (1960), p. 57.

59 *Ibid.*

60 Snodland Historical Society website, http://www.snodlandhistory.org.uk/index.htm.

61 Interview with Robert Coomber at Snodland Museum, Sunday 15 November 2009.

62 Margary, Ivan D, 'The North Downs Main Trackway and the Pilgrims' Way', *Archaeological Journal Volume 109*, p. 49.

63 Manorial Records, Manor of the Bishop of Rochester – Medway Archives, 1202–1754; Halling with appertances of Cuxton and Holborough, 8 April 1720.

64 Hasted, Edward, *The History and Topographical Survey of the County of Kent*, Volume 3 (1797), pp. 481–98.

65 Belloc, *op. cit.*, p. 249.

66 *Ibid.*, p. 250.

67 Phelps, Rev. Henry Dampier, *Notes on Snodland Volume III – History, Flora and Fauna* (Snodland Historical Society, 2005), p. 13.

68 Hasted, Edward, *The History and Topographical Survey of the County of Kent*, Volume 4 (1798), pp. 463–47.

69 Belloc, *op. cit.*, p. 244.

70 *Ibid.*, p. 245.

71 *Ibid.*

72 Margary, Ivan, 'The North Downs Main Trackway and the Pilgrims' Way', *Archaeological Journal Volume 109*, p. 49.

73 Jusserand, J.J., *English Wayfaring Life in the Middle Ages* (1909), p. 65, footnote quoting Stow's *Annales* (London, 1631), p. 201.

74 Webb, Diana, *Pilgrimage in Medieval England* (Hambledown & London, 2000), p. 228, making reference to N. Yates & J. Gibson, *Traffic and Politics: The Construction and Management of Rochester Bridge, AD 43–1993* (Woodbridge, 1994). In the eyre roll of 1292–94 the deaths of *quidam peregrine ignoti* are recorded (p. 39, n. 98).

75 Jennett, Sean, *The Pilgrims' Way – from Winchester to Canterbury* (Cassell & Co., 1971), p. 211.

76 Finch, William Coles, *In Kentish Pilgrims Land* (C.W. Daniel Co., 1925), p. 202.

8 Population and Pilgrimage

1 Elliston-Erwood, F.C., 'The Pilgrims' Way, its antiquity and its alleged medieval use', *Archaeologia Cantiana Volume 37* (1925), p. 1.

2 Elliston-Erwood, F.C., *The Pilgrims Road* (The Homeland Association, 1923), p. 37.

3 Crump, C.G., 'The Pilgrims' Way', *History Quarterly* (June 1936), p. 22.

4 *Ibid.*, quoting from Dr Peter Brieger's article in *History* (June 1935) entitled 'Relations in History, Geography and Art'.

5 *Ibid.*, p. 24.

6 James, Captain E. Renouard, *Notes on the Pilgrims Way in West Surrey* (London: Edward Stanford, 1871), p. 6.

7 *Ibid.*, p.7

8 Cartwright, Julia, *The Pilgrims' Way – from Winchester to Canterbury* (first published 1893, this edition, Wildwood House, 1982), p. 5.

9 Belloc, Hilaire, *The Old Road* (1911), p. 91.

10 Finch, William Coles, *In Kentish Pilgrims Land* (1925), p. 77, makes reference to A.S. Lamprey, MA, *Guide to Maidstone*, p. 3.

11 Hooper, Wilfred, ILD, 'The Pilgrims' Way and its supposed pilgrim use', *Surrey Archaeological Collections Volume 44* (1936), p. 56.

12 Webb, Diana, *Pilgrimage in Medieval England* (Hambledon & London, 2000), p. 181.

13 Gairdner, James (ed.), *The Paston Letters AD 1422–1509*, Volume 5, New Complete Library Edition (Constable, 1904), p. 112.

14 Nilson, Ben, *Shrine Accounts and offerings from Cathedral Shrines and Medieval England* (Boydell & Brewer Inc.), p. 147.

15 Elliston-Erwood, F.C., 'The Pilgrims' Way, its antiquity and its alleged medieval use', *Archaeologia Cantiana Volume 37* (1925), p. 15.

16 Mortimer, Ian, *Time Traveller's Guide to Medieval England* (Vintage, 2009), describes villeins as unfree peasants and states that 'villeins work the lord's land for him' and that 'those who are not free are villeins and bondmen'.

17 Sumption, Jonathan, *Pilgrimage* (Faber & Faber, 2002), p. 165.

18 Webb, Diana, *Pilgrimage in Medieval England* (Hambledon & London, 2000), p. 231.

19 *op. cit.*, p. 232.

20 Bartlett, Robert, *England Under the Norman and Angevin Kings 1075–1225* (Oxford: Clarendon Press, 2000), pp. 290–4.

21 Darby, H.C., 'Domesday England', *A New Historical Geography of England* (Cambridge University Press, 1977), p. 87.

22 Domesday population estimates using the conventional multiplier of 5: *Ibid.*, pp. 33, 45, 54.
23 Palmer, J. et al., *Electronic Edition of Domesday Book: Translation, Databases and Scholarly Commentary, 1086* (computer file), Colchester, Essex: UK Data Archive (distributor), September 2007. SN: 5694.
24 Jusserand, J.J., *English Wayfaring Life in the Middle Ages* (1909), pp. 257–8.
25 Bartlett, Robert, *England under the Norman and Angevin Kings 1075–1225* (Oxford: Clarendon Press, 2000), p. 324.
26 Mortimer, Ian, *A Time Traveller's Guide to Medieval England* (Vintage, 2009), p. 68.
27 Jusserand, *op. cit.*, p. 258.
28 *Ibid.*, p. 261.
29 Schofield, Philip R., *Peasant and Community on Medieval England 1200–15* (Palgrave Macmillan, 2003), p. 3.
30 Sumption, Jonathan, *Pilgrimage* (Faber & Faber, 2002), p. 165.
31 Darby, H.C., 'Domesday England', *A New Historical Geography of England* (Cambridge University Press, 1977), p. 89; and Bartlett, Robert, *England under the Norman and Angevin Kings 1075–1225*, (Oxford: Clarendon Press, 2000), p. 291.
32 Bartlett, Robert, *Ibid.*, p. 324.
33 Hatcher, 'Plague Population', from Mortimer, Ian, 2009.
34 Russell, Josiah Cox, *British Medieval Population*, Table of Crude Expectation Ages 1–20a (University of New Mexico, 1948), p. 176.

9 Conclusion

1 Hooper, Wilfrid, ILD, 'The Pilgrims' Way and its supposed use', *Surrey Archaeological Collections Volume 44* (1936), p. 76.
2 Belloc, *op. cit.*, 1921, p. 4.
3 Cartwright, *op. cit.*, p. 2.

Bibliography

Adair, John, *The Pilgrims' Way – Shrines and Saints in Britain and Ireland* (Book Club Associates, 1978).

Allen, Grant, *Science in Arcady* (Lawrence & Bullen, 1892).

Bartlett, Robert, *England under the Norman and Angevin Kings 1075–1225* (Clarenden Press, 2000).

Belloc, Hilaire, *The Old Road* (Archibald Constable & Co., 1904).

———, *The Old Road* (first published 1904, this edition Constable & Co., 1921).

Belsey, Valerie, *The Green Lanes of England* (Green Books, 1998).

Brandon, Peter, *The Kent and Sussex Weald* (Phillimore, 2003).

———, *The North Downs* (Phillimore, 2005).

Brayley, Edward Wedlake, *A Topographical History of Surrey Volume IV* (G. Willis, 1850).

Brookes, Stuart & Harrington, Sue, *The Kingdom and People of Kent AD 400–1066* (The History Press, 2010).

Bunyan, John, *The Pilgrims' Progress* (The Religious Tract Society).

Calow, David, 'Investigation of a possible Roman road at Bighton and Medstead', *Hampshire Field Club Newsletter* 53 (autumn 2010).

Cartwright, Julia, *The Pilgrims' Way – from Winchester to Canterbury* (first published in GB 1893, this edition re-issued Wildwood House, 1982).

———, *The Pilgrims' Way – from Winchester to Canterbury* (J.S. Virtue & Co., 1893).

———, *The Pilgrims' Way – from Winchester to Canterbury* (revised edition, John Murray, 1911).

Charles, Alan, *Exploring the Pilgrims' Way* (Countryside Books, 1990).

Chaucer, Geoffrey, *The Canterbury Tales* (Penguin Popular Classics, 1996).

Cobbett, William, *Rural Rides Volume 1 and 2* (Everyman's Library, first published in this edition 1912, this edition 1932).

Cochrane, C., *The Lost Roads of Wessex* (Pan Books, 1972).

Coles, Finch William, *In Kentish Pilgrims Land* (C.W. Daniel Co., 1925).

Crump, C.G., 'The Pilgrims' Way', *History Quarterly* (June 1936).

Darby, H.C., *Domesday England* (Cambridge University Press, 1977).

Elliston-Erwood, F.C., 'The Pilgrims' Way, its antiquity and its alleged mediaeval use', *Archaeologia Cantiana Volume 37* (1925).

Elliston-Erwood, F.C., 'Miscellaneous Notes on some Kent Roads and allied matters', *Archaeologia Cantiana Volume 70* (1956).

———, *The Pilgrims' Road* (The Riverside Press Ltd, first published 1910, this edition 1923).

Furley Robert, FSA, *A History of the Weald of Kent Volume One* (Henry Igglesden, 1871).

———, *A History of the Weald of Kent Volume Two* (Henry Igglesden, 1874).

Goodsall, Robert H., *The Ancient Road to Canterbury – A Progress through Kent* (Constable, 1960).

Gough, Henry, *Itinerary of King Edward the First throughout his reign,* AD *1272–1307* (Alexander Gardner, 1900).

Hart, Edwin, FSA, 'The Pilgrims' Way from Shere to Titsey as traced by public records and remains', *Surrey Archaeological Collections Volume 41* (1936).

Hippisley, Cox R., *The Green Roads of England* (first published 1914, this edition, Methuen & Co., 1948).

Hooper, Wilfrid, 'The Pilgrims' Way and its supposed use', *Surrey Archaeological Collections Volume 44* (1936).

James, Captain E. Renouard, *Notes on the Pilgrims' Way in West Surrey* (Edward Stanford, 1871).

Jennett, Sean, *The Pilgrims' Way – from Winchester to Canterbury* (Cassell & Co., 1971).

Jessop, R.F., *The Archaeology of Kent* (Methuen, 1930).

Jusserand, J.J., *English Wayfaring Life in the Middle Ages* (first published 1888, this edition, T. Fisher Unwin, 1909).

Knocker, Captain H.W., 'The Valley of Holmesdale – its evolution and development', *Archaeologia Cantiana Volume 31* (1915).

Langland, *Piers the Ploughman* (Penguin Classics, 1975).

Lawson, T. & Killingray, D. (eds), *An Historical Atlas of Kent* (Phillimore & Co., 2004).

Laxton, Howard, *Pilgrimage to Canterbury* (David & Charles, 1978).

Margary, Ivan D., 'The North Downs Main Trackway and the Pilgrims' Way', *Archaeological Journal Volume 119* (1952).

Massingham, H.J., *English Downland* (B.T.Batsford Ltd, first published 1936, this edition 1942–43).

Moncrief, A.R., *Hope, The Pilgrims' Way* (London, 1906).

Mortimer, Ian, *The Time Traveller's Guide to Medieval England* (Vintage, 2009).

Nilson, Ben, *Cathedral Shrines of Medieval England* (Boydell Press, 2001).

Ohler, Norbert, *The Medieval Traveller* (Boydell Press, 1989).

Rackham, Oliver, *The Illustrated History of the Countryside* (first published 1994, this edition, Phoenix, 1997).

Ravensdale, Jack, *In the Steps of Chaucer's Pilgrims* (Guild Publishing, 1989).

Schofield, Philip R., *Peasant and Community on Medieval England 1200–1500* (Palgrave Macmillan, 2003).

Stanley, Arthur P., *Historical Memorials of Canterbury* (1855).

Sumption, Jonathan, *Pilgrimage*, first published (Faber & Faber, 1975, this edition 2002).

Taylor, Christopher, *Roads and Tracks of Britain* (Orion, 1994).

Thornhill, Patrick, 'The Medway Crossings of the Pilgrims' Way', *Archaeologia Cantiana Volume 89* (1974).

Timperley, H.W. & Brill, Edith, *Ancient Trackways of Wessex* (Nonsuch, first published 1965, this edition 2005).

Tuson, Dan, *The Kent Downs* (Tempus, 2007).

Ure, John, *Pilgrimages – The Great Adventure of the Middle Age* (Carroll & Graff, 2006).

Ward, H. Snowden, *The Canterbury Pilgrimages* (Adam & Charles Black, 1904).

Watt, Francis, *Canterbury Pilgrims and their Way* (Methuen & Co. Ltd, 1917).

Way, Albert, 'The Pilgrims' Way or Path towards the Shrine of St Thomas of Canterbury' in Stanley, Arthur P., *Historical Memorials of Canterbury* (London: John Murray, 1855).

Webb, Diana, *Pilgrimage in Medieval England* (Hambledon & London, 2000).

Weston, David, 'Roman Roads East of Winchester I', *Hampshire Field Club Newsletter* 49 (spring 2008).

Williams, John H., *The Archaeology of Kent to AD 800* (Boydell Press, 2007).

Wright, Christopher John, *A Guide to the Pilgrims' Way and North Downs Way, A Constable Guide* (first published in GB 1971, this edition 1985).

Index

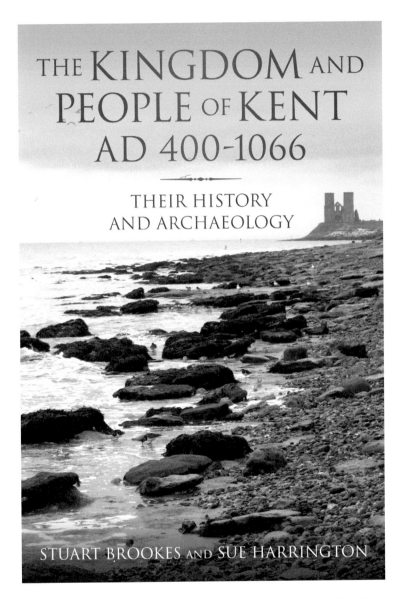

THE KINGDOM AND PEOPLE OF KENT AD 400-1066

THEIR HISTORY AND ARCHAEOLOGY

STUART BROOKES AND SUE HARRINGTON

The Kingdom and People of Kent: Their History and Archaeology

Stuart Brookes & Sue Harrington

978 0 7524 5694 2

www.thehistorypress.co.uk

The History Press

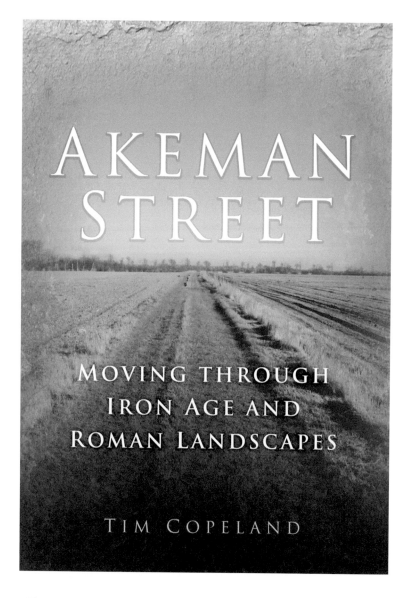

Akeman Street: Moving Through Iron Age and Roman Landscapes

Tim Copeland

978 0 7524 1958 9

www.thehistorypress.co.uk